WILL THE
REAL PHONY
PLEASE STAND UP
BY ETHEL BARRETT

A Division of G/L Publications
Glendale, California, U. S. A.

Over 215,000 in print

Second Printing, 1969
Third Printing, 1969
Fourth Printing, 1970
Fifth Printing, 1971
Sixth Printing, 1971

© Copyright 1969 by G/L Publications
All Rights Reserved
Printed in U.S.A.

Published by
Regal Books Division, G/L Publications
Glendale, California 91209 U.S.A.

Library of Congress Catalog Card No. 69-19873

ISBN 8307-0041-2

Contents

A teaching and discussion guide for use with this book is available from your church supplier.

Which James?
What Letter?

Which James? Why the head of the church at Jerusalem, of course. He was the head man there at Paul's last visit (Acts 21:18). Paul calls him a "Special Messenger" (Galatians 1:19). If you'd lived back in the 40's (the years 40 to 50, that is) you'd have heard him discussed by the Sheep Gate of Jerusalem, or in the funny crooked streets, or in the shade of the Temple porches, or in the Court of the Gentiles within the Temple itself.

For he was an immensely important and influential man—known as "James the Just." When he spoke people listened and when he said "jump" people said "how high?"

Pretty lofty, that. But weren't there others in the same position? What about Paul? And John? And Peter? Paul saw Jesus on the road to Damascus. John was known as the "disciple Jesus loved." Peter took Jesus' hand and walked with Him on the water.

But James had a unique distinction that none of the others could claim. James was our Lord's brother. Not figuratively. Actually. His "born-and-brought-up" brother. Jesus was Mary's son by the Holy Spirit of God and James was Mary's son by Joseph. He ate at the same table with Jesus, worked in the same carpenter's shop with Him, went to the synagogue with Him, grew up with Him.

And knew Him as the Son of God? Not for a minute. For James did not recognize the glorious truth when it was right under his nose. The Bible is replete with evidence that Jesus' family neither understood nor believed on Him.

How many times James must have been scandalized at the things his brother was doing! Turning water into wine at Cana. Hobnobbing with that no-good Zacchaeus, denouncing the Pharisees (James *was* one), eating with Publicans and sinners, befriending a woman like Mary Magdalene, stopping to chat with a Samaritan woman by the side of a well, preaching to the hoi polloi on a hillside! Outrageous! James must have spent a good deal of his life apologizing for his brother Jesus. Right up until His ignominious and shameful death.

And then our Lord rose from the dead. And "He was seen of James." Paul tells us this. Nothing more. The rest is locked in mystery. Jesus was seen of James somewhere, and whatever happened, James was sent spinning, his soul shaken to the foundations, his life never to be the same. Jesus was never his brother again. Jesus was his Lord.

And so when James came to write the letter, he did not begin by saying: "From James, the eminent, most right-right Reverend, the brother of Jesus."

He began by saying: "From James, a servant of God and of the Lord Jesus Christ, the Lord of Glory."

What letter? Why the letter that was written to the Jewish Christians that had been scattered into the provinces by persecution, by circumstances, by hardship. The letter was to buck them up, bawl them out, remind them of both their privileges and responsibilities, and, in general, jolt them out of their doldrums and into reality.

What a thundering letter it is!

He begins with a smashing paradox: "You've got problems? Then be happy" (1:2)! That's enough to stand anybody on his ear. He flings out rhetorical questions and carries on imaginary conversations: "If you have a friend in need and you say to him 'God bless you' and then don't help him, what good does that do" (2:14-16)? He thunders imperatives ("Do it or else!") and they are scattered in abundance throughout his letter. He turns without warning to the particular "groups": "Look here, you rich men!" He uses pictures from everyday life: "A great forest can be set on fire by one tiny spark" (3:6). And examples of famous men and women: "Don't you remember that even our father Abraham . . ." (2:21)? He fires searching questions at his hapless readers: "So what right do you have to judge or criticize others?" All in all, and with every trick he knows, he is saying, *"Get going!"*

He leaps without apology from one subject to another. And a book could be written about any one of them. It's a bit like Wiley's dictionary. Wiley (a character in a comic strip) worked hard and long writing a dictionary. And two of his friends had a bit to say about it: "I just read Wiley's novel."

"That isn't a novel. It's a dictionary."

"Oh. Well I *thought* the plot was a bit choppy in spots."

It's "a bit choppy in spots," all right. But you'll like it that way. For it's a blazing collection of truths, challenges, questions, arguments, and merciless probings, dissecting every facet of your personality and intruding into every area of your life.

And through it all is an outraged cry against the great bug-a-boo of Christianity—*hypocrisy*.

Wherever Christianity does not mean *love*, wherever church ritual is not related to *life*, wherever the needs of others are ignored, wherever Christians' jargon is denied by their *lives*, this letter is pertinent and up-to-date and very much *"now."*

Oh, yes. James was known as "the man with the camel's knees," his knees were so calloused and hardened by much kneeling in prayer.

His "practical Christianity" was not amiss either. Tradition has it that he was thrown from the top of the Temple and then stoned to death. He must have practiced what he preached to invite a fate like that. His Christianity must have been as outrageously "for real" as his brother's had been.

It's a great roaring letter written by a great roaring man. If you want to get a good look at the phonies around you, you'll enjoy reading it—with great roaring relish.

And here and there, you just *might* get a fleeting glimpse of yourself.

1
Into each life
some rain must fall

INTO EACH LIFE
SOME RAIN
MUST FALL
...BUT THIS IS RIDICULOUS!

It's one of the signs you can find in a card rack. People collect them to send to friends or tack up behind their desks. These signs appeal to us and tickle us, not only because they are kooky but because underneath the laugh is a basic truth that hurts; they tell us how we really feel. Any analysis of humor will tell us that it is serious business, a twist on the problems we are all heir to, from minor problems to tragedies. The core of humor is always the same; somebody's in a bind. And because each of us is in more or less of a bind most of the time, we identify.

Your first problem loomed its ugly head when you were in a basket: How to get attention. There you were, wrapped in folds of comfort with your stomach full and your diaper dry. But everyone else in your world had gone off to the far-flung shores of the kitchen or the living room or (horrors!) even the yard. But you were born with a built-in computer to tell you how to get what you wanted. So "Gas!" you bellowed, or "Pin!" whichever came handily to mind, and the truants came arunning to snap to attention and pick you up.

Your next big problem probably came when you were imprisoned in a playpen looking at the world of lucky adults through humiliating bars. To sit there in ignominious defeat was plainly intolerable, and sooner or later, depending on your perserverance, you learned to climb out. To do anything less would have made you a rank coward; you would never have been able to face yourself.

As you grew older the problems grew tougher. Plainly, there was only one solution; change your circumstances. So off you went to school, heady with new dreams, clean slate and all that sort of thing, your "Show-and-Tell" already composed and memorized. And the first thing you ran into was "You mustn't do that," and "We love to share, don't we?" and "Don't hit Janie because she doesn't like you, just go play with somebody *else*."

This was going to be grim business.

But incredibly it came to pass that you grew up and survived those humiliating years, and the awful problems of adolescence are past, and the driver's test, and the monumental battle of winning people's confidence and respect, so you are now reasonably certain that your mother won't sew name tapes on your clothes when you go on your honeymoon. And now you are practically an adult by the standards of our civilization, and more of an adult in many areas than some adults you know, and you have at long last learned one incontrovertible truth.

Problems are here to stay.

Problems are not only here to stay but they manage to keep up with the times. This enables you to remind your elders of the fact that *they* did not have the problems *you* have in these complicated computerized days, and thereby throw everybody into utter confusion so you can mope in peace or go off in a snit. The truth is that problems come custom-made and couched in different terminology for each generation but basically they are the same old culprits.

This would be discouraging business except for one fact: God's answers are in the Bible. Just as they always were. He knew the electronic age was coming; He hasn't slipped up on anything. And He knew you before you were born and every gene and chromosome that was going into the making of your own unique and complex self, and in what combinations. He also knew what your problems were going to be and He's counting on your intelligence to recognize the fact that no matter how they are couched, in the age you're living in, they are basically the same old gadflies buzzing in your face and impeding your progress if you don't "Watch it."

Problems are a fact: how do I face them?

With this great truth (or dreary business, depending on how you feel) in mind, let's look at the Book of James.

1"James, a servant of God and of the Lord Jesus Christ, sends greeting to the twelve dispersed tribes."

And then you'd expect some small talk, some preliminaries, some buildup for the bombshell that follows. But James drops it in the second verse.

2"When all kinds of trials and temptations crowd into your lives, my brothers, don't resent them as intruders, but welcome them as friends!"

This is a stunning blow. Surely God could not have meant it. If you are a reasonable person you might want to give God the benefit of the doubt and look up the same verse in the Authorized Version; perhaps the modern translator made a mistake. But there you find the words "count it all joy."

Sure enough, it meant what it said.

Now this is enough to make you wrap up your accoutrements in an old shirt and head for the nearest Walden Pond where there might conceivably be no problems, you hope. Here James is talking about problems from the *outside*. The word "temptations" in this instance means testing. As God's child, you are to be *tested*. When God led the Israelites into the Promised Land, He did not remove the enemies who were there; He left them so the Israelites might be *tested* in their struggle against them. So in this verse, the problems he means were not of your doing. They bolted out of the blue and drenched you in despair or left you squirming and helpless with resignation or rage, as the case may be. How can *you* help alcoholic parents or a disease that left you maimed or the betrayal of a friend or the fender that got dented in the family car while you were driving and it wasn't your fault or the fact that summer jobs are nigh impossible to find or people who aren't Christians and don't understand you or people who *are* Christians and don't understand you or poverty or your race or unfair treatment from teachers or bosses or whatever? Count it all joy indeed. Monstrous. It would seem that God is an ogre after all.

But wait. Read it again. It does not say that all *is* joy. Or that "Happiness is problems" like "Happiness is a warm puppy." To say that would be fraudulent. And misguided Christians who tell us that from the moment we accept Christ and become Christians, life is going to be all joy pure joy from there on out, are leaving us wide open for disillusionment and confusion the moment the first problem rears its ugly head. Problems are not happiness. And problems are not pure joy. And the verse does not say so. It says "welcome them" and in the King James, *"count* it all joy."

Well this isn't much better. We seem to have gotten the verse all clear only to fog it up again. Welcome them? Count it all joy? In the name of common sense, why? There's got to be a reason. There is.

What's in it for me?

It doesn't seem like a very polite question and the longer you are a Christian (if you're growing, that

6

is) the less inclined you are to ask it. But the truth of the matter is, there *is* something in it for you. With God there always is. You simply cannot lose for winning. He'll outdo, outgive and outsmart you every time.

When God tells you to be happy and count it all joy, He is telling you to look at it from the positive side; the wretched problem just *could* be turned into profit. And the one who profits just could be *you*. Read on.

"Realize that they come to test your faith and to produce in you the quality of endurance."

Not much of a challenge here. On the face of it, "endurance" sounds a bit namby-pamby, rather like the insipid smiles of bad religious art. Could give you just that sort of a smile, too, punctuated with little sighs and fluttering gestures, your martyr complex all aglow, signifying that you feel so noble you can hardly stand it. But the Greek word does not denote a namby-pamby passive quality at all; the Greek word is vibrant and dynamic; it denotes *staying power*, it's a "don't quit" word.

Other things being equal, the attribute that makes a champion is endurance. He keeps on going, sometimes after all the indications are that he is licked. He just won't *quit*.

Admittedly we're not all champs; most of us are pluggers. But anyone who has ever gone on an exercise program (and stuck to it) knows the discouraging drag. The cramps, the sore muscles begging you to quit, until, if you won't, they do. "Enough!" they bellow, after twenty-five times, and

7

that leg just won't go up on the count of twenty-six. But you plug away each morning, determined that "one of these days—" And then it happens. Twenty-six, twenty-seven, twenty-eight—incredible! Twenty-nine, thirty—fantastic! Thirty-one, thirty-two—

and all the way up to fifty without a hitch! You would have been happy to get to twenty-six, but you *doubled* it! Why the sudden jump? How? Medical research tells us that a whole network of blood vessels feeding those muscles has been developing to take care of the extra demand, and when it finally opened for operation, it opened, not one vessel at a time, but the whole network at once, like a new freeway leading to the boondocks! So while you were plugging away, with no apparent sign of progress, you were developing like mad without even knowing it. Read on.

"But let the process go on until that endurance is fully developed, and you will find you have become men of mature character with the right sort of independence."

What is God up to?

He's trying your "staying power," your endurance, to be sure. But why? What's the point? The real issue at stake here is your faith. Through your problems, your patience is getting a chance to grow, but it's your faith that is being tested. Is it "for real"? If it isn't, there's nothing like a man-sized problem to put a little strain on it and show it up for what it is.

"But why? Doesn't God already know my faith?" Of course He does. But He wants *you* to find out what it is, and He wants it to *mature*. Your staying power is in direct proportion to your faith; they grow together. And while you are persevering, whole new "networks" of strength, like the blood vessels, are developing undercover, and you are progressing like mad without even knowing it. The whole process is painful; it would be foolish to say it is not. But you didn't get those rippling muscles and lean body by swinging in a hammock either. Muscle tone doesn't grow by neglect; it doesn't even stay around very long. You can take it for granted for a while, but that day of reckoning comes, inexorably, and you wake up to find you are all flab, have been all flab for some time. You got flabby by degrees, and didn't notice it.

So let your staying power (and your faith) grow. Then, as James says, you'll be strong in character, really mature.

I'm willing but nothing works

"At this point you've furrowed my brow. Faith? I
not only have faith as big as a mustard seed, I think
I have faith as big as an acre of mustard plants. I
believe God implicitly. I believe that Jesus is Christ
the Lord, the Son of God. I've asked Him to be *my*
Lord. I'm realistic enough to realize that the Christian life is *not* problem free. And I go along with
the whole concept. I don't resent it and I'm not
fighting against it. As far as I know, my faith is okay
and my heart is willing. But my problems have
teeth in them. They're big and they're for real. I've
tried everything I know, but I don't seem to be able
to compute; the right answer won't come out. I
think I have the courage; where do I get the know-
how?"

Of course. God knew you were going to ask this.
The answer is in the Bible. Next verse.

"'And if, in the process, any of you does not
know how to meet any particular problem he has
only to ask God—who gives generously to all men
without making them feel foolish or guilty—and he
may be quite sure that the necessary wisdom will
be given him.'"

James might have told you this right off, but he
was building up to it. You had to realize that problems were profitable to you, first, before you'd
scream for help.

"But wait. Isn't this too easy? I want to do things
on my own; I'm conditioned to it. All my upbring-
ing has taught me to 'do it myself.'" If you're the
type that relishes a good fight, you still have it.

10

Reread the verse. It doesn't say if you want to know how God will handle it—it says if you want to know how God wants *you* to handle it, just ask Him. That's no namby-pamby verse; it has blood and sinew in it; cut it and it bleeds. If you want a challenge, it beats painting a sign and running off to a protest rally any day.

All right, you have that straight. And you're willing to ask God. But wait. There's a proviso, it's in the next three verses. *BUT.*

⁴"But he must ask in sincere faith without secret doubts as to whether he really wants God's help or not. The man who trusts God, but with inward reservations, is like a wave of the sea, carried forward by the wind one moment and driven back the next. ⁷That sort of man cannot hope to receive anything from the Lord, ⁸and the life of a man of divided loyalty will reveal instability at every turn."

Ah, so easy to say, so hard to do. All of our nature militates against it. Admittedly, the proviso is a big one. And yet it's so simple. Believe God. If you keep dwelling only on the problem, or give Him the problem and then take it back, or let your mind flit back and forth from His greatness to your own inadequate self, your mind will split in two, each part in conflict with the other. As an old Jewish Rabbi said, "Let not those who pray have two hearts, one directed to God, one to something else." You'll wind up in helpless confusion, tossed about like a wave changing from moment to moment as the wind blows on it.

But how do you "unsplit" your mind? How do you

11

get this kind of faith so that you can ask with no reservations, with no doubts, with no wavering? And what of the people who tell you they *always* have this kind of faith? Don't let them discourage you. The fact that they boast makes them suspect. Either they haven't encountered a problem monumental enough to put a strain on their faith, or they are fudging a bit somewhere. The plain truth is, you don't have this kind of faith on your own and you can't conjure it up. You really try, but it's no go; you wind up spinning your wheels. Which leaves you right back where you started from. What to do? Is there an answer? There is.

God knew you were apt to run into this little dilemma and He didn't leave you dangling. He never does. He gave you an example in Mark 9. A man came to Jesus with an apparently insoluble problem and Jesus said to him, "If you can believe, all things are possible to him that believes," and the man cried out and said with tears, "Lord, I believe—" and then he felt himself flounder and his mind split in two and he didn't try to fool himself or to pretend to be "spiritual" in front of the crowd; he decided to be honest and he cried out, "*Help thou mine unbelief!*" What a statement! It warms your heart. The uncluttered simplicity of his attitude makes you want to say "Bravo." And it got results. Read Mark 9:17-27 and you'll get the whole story. It's a great one. Jesus actually *gave* him the faith he asked for. But he had to admit he needed it.

Specifically what do I do?

Talk to God about your problem. Read His Word

12

and meditate on it. Ask Him to help you get the problem in the right perspective. State it aloud. If it's still muddled, write it down. Don't edit or distort or change or evade; state it as it is. *Do all this with the determination that you are going to obey.* Although obedience is not mentioned, it is implicit throughout these verses. "If any man willeth to do His will, he shall know of the teaching" (John 7:17, A.R.V.).

Once this is done, amazing things will begin to happen. Now you will look at the culprit, not emotionally, trapped in your own feelings, but objectively, as if you'd stepped outside the whole wretched business and are viewing it without judgment or passion—just trying to see it for what it is. Now, if you really mean business, you might see if and how *you* might be contributing to it, or sabotaging its resolution. Now, if you are really looking at it objectively, self-pity has *got* to go. And resentment. And the determination to have your own way in the matter at any cost. And all the negative attitudes that were tripping you up. Now you can put it in God's hands. Doesn't He know about it? Didn't He (assuming you did not create it yourself) give it to you? Doesn't He have a purpose? And doesn't He care? In the face of all this, the idea that the thing is hopeless is unthinkable. It is *profitable*—and you're the one who is going to reap the profits.

Your problems are custom-made

In verses 9-11 are the two extremes—the person who "wasn't there" when all the gifts were given out, and the "guy who has everything."

⁹"The brother who is poor may be glad because God has called him to the true riches. ¹⁰The rich may be glad that God has shown him his spiritual poverty. For the rich man, as such, will wither away as surely as summer flowers. ¹¹One day the sunrise brings a scorching wind; the grass withers at once and so do all the flowers—all that lovely sight is destroyed. Just as surely will the rich man and all his extravagant ways fall into the blight of decay."

Are you poor? Are you lacking in money, in talent, in looks, in opportunities, in "the breaks"? Rejoice! You are of great worth to God. You are of worth in the church, in the world. You are rich, rich, you are a child of the *King*. *God* is your Father. Rejoice in the things you *cannot lose*.

Are you rich? Money can be lost, talent can be snatched away, looks can fade, circumstances can change for the worse. Happy are you if you are aware of this. Rejoice in the things you *cannot lose*.

In between these two extremes lies every conceivable combination of circumstances, gifts, talents, "breaks." And no matter where you are on the scale you will have problems, and they are custom-made for you.

You are uniquely *you;* there is nobody else who has ever been born who is quite like you. And the testings God sends into your life are to meet *your* needs, show you *your* weaknesses, develop *your* character. To give a problem a name (broken home, handicap, disease, poverty, betrayal, gossip mongers, etc.) and pop it into a category and then go down in fear under its onslaught is to stumble

over semantics; you are afraid of *words*. And the
words might not mean exactly the same thing in
your case as they do in other cases, for even if the
circumstances seem the same, *you* are different. So
in the last analysis, it's just you and your problem—
and God.

There's more to it than meets the eye

If you don't believe it, read the Book of Job. In
the prologue we find that Job's problems were all
planned in the councils of heaven before he ever
knew he was going to have them. And in the epilogue we find that their final outcome was a *blessing*.

In between these two points we have a group
therapy session, in this case a group of wiseacres
pooling their ignorance. Their theorizing and
philosophizing are learned and eloquent as far as
they go. But because they are doing it from incom-
plete premises they can go nowhere but around in
circles. The prologue and epilogue are the *unknown
quantities* and it isn't until Job turns his eyes to God
that the whole thing makes sense.

There's more to your problem than meets the eye;
just trust God for the prologue and epilogue. If you
could see the complete picture there would be no
room for faith. God keeps just enough from you to
give your faith a little growing room! I Peter 1:6,7
tells us: "There is wonderful joy ahead, even though
the going is rough for a while down here. These
trials are only to test your faith [that you may] see
whether or not it is strong and pure" *(Living New
Testament)*.

15

A girl burst into her pastor's study one time, and in her middle-sized voice said, "I have a question."

"Yes?" he said.

"Why is it," she said in her great big voice, "that some people just seem to be born in the right family, go to the right school, marry the right person, have the right children, and never seem to have any problems?"

The pastor looked at her for a moment. Then he said softly, "But they don't grow."

"But they *do!*" she said in her middle-sized voice. "The ones I'm thinking of do!"

"Then they have problems," he said. "They just don't show."

"Oh," she said in her teeny-weeny voice. And she left. There was nothing more to say.

Think

1. Read I Peter 4:12-19. Write down a problem (yours). Examine it in the light of verse 15 and see if you are snitching a bit. Now examine it in the light of verse 19. Does it honestly fit into this category? If it does, carry on!

2. Read Psalm 142:1-7. Are you depending on people only to solve your problems? Remember, you can't be disappointed in a person *unless you are leaning on him to the exclusion of God.*

3. Memorize Romans 8:28. Can you list any ways in which your problem might work out for your good? If you can't, can you trust God for it? (or for the unknown quantity?)

2
Temptation,
thy name is trouble

Thou dost bring us nothing but grief, and surely no good ever comes of thee—but why oh why art thou so *attractive?*

Yes indeed.

The dictionary tells us that "tempt" means: *To allure or entice to something unwise or wicked. To induce or persuade by enticement or allurement, as to do something unwise or wrong. To attract by holding out the probability of gratification or advantage, often in the direction of that which is wrong or unwise.*

18

And James has dwelt on this business of temptation at considerable length:

James 1:12-18

[12]"The man who patiently endures the temptations and trials that come to him is the truly happy
man. For once his testing is complete he will receive the crown of life which the Lord has promised
to all who love him.

[13]"A man must not say when he is tempted, 'God
is tempting me.' For God cannot be tempted by
evil, and does not himself tempt anyone. [14]No, a
man's temptation is due to the pull of his own inward desires, which can be enormously attractive.
[15]His own desire takes hold of him, and that produces sin. And sin in the long run means death—
[16]make no mistake about that, brothers of mine!
[17]But every good endowment that we possess and
every complete gift that we have received must
come from above, from the Father of all lights, with
whom there is never the slightest variation or shadow of inconsistency. [18]By his own wish he made us
his own sons through the Word of truth, that we
might be, so to speak, the first specimens of his new
creation."

In verse fourteen, the authorized version says,
"But every man is tempted when he is drawn away
of his own lust, and *enticed.*" And James is using a
metaphor taken from hunting and fishing; to lure
forth the game from its covert, to entice a fish with
the bait. And it goes without saying that the game
so lured and the fish so enticed did not stay around
long enough to make any plans.

TEMPTATION!
WHAT A LURE...

To take the bait meant disaster. In any case, temptation has been around for a long time and it's here to stay. What a wretched business.

UNTIL YOU SWALLOW IT

Let's blame it all on God

Psychologists tell us that one of the main characteristics of the four-year-old is blaming others for the messes he gets into. "I didn't do it—*he* did it!" he bellows, and that seems to settle everything.

It's an understandable trait that we all had at that tender age and it would be all right if we'd got over it, like the measles, but unfortunately we never do, entirely. We still have this proclivity to a greater or lesser degree, right up until our heads are hoary and our spines are shrinking and we jolly well should know better.

Well, why *not* blame God? It's the easy way out, and seems quite logical. He created everything; He must have thought up temptation too.

Omar Khayyam thought so:

O Thou who didst with pitfall and with gin,
    Beset the path I was to wander in—

Robert Burns thought so:

Thou knowest Thou hast formed me
    With passions wild and strong:
And listening to their witching voice
    Has often led me wrong.

They concluded that their conduct was all God's fault; He had created them the way they were; let Him make the best of it!

But James tells us emphatically: "A man must not say when he is tempted, 'God is tempting me.' For God cannot be tempted by evil, and does not himself tempt anyone."

Then who? And why?

It started back in the Garden of Eden. And the culprit was Satan. "Has God told you you could not eat the fruit of every tree in the garden?" Satan asked Eve, and the implication was obvious; here was something Eve could not have. "Every tree but one," said Eve. "God has told us not to eat of it or touch it, or we will die." And Satan came up with the very first temptation and it was most attractive and enticing. "You won't *surely* die," he said, "God knows if you eat it your eyes shall be opened and you shall be as gods."

The rest is history. She ate it. She gave some to Adam. He ate it. And immediately the talent for blaming someone else came to them, full-blown. When God confronted Adam with his sin, Adam said, "She's to blame." And when God confronted Eve, she said, "The serpent's to blame."

And there we have it. But is it a bit too pat? Doesn't it follow that if God created Adam and Eve and they did what they did—that He created evil?

No, God did not create evil. He created man and gave him free will. Well, we argue, man *chose* evil; isn't it the same thing? No it isn't. And it all has to do with love. God's love for you is a wonderful and mysterious thing. The wonder of it is that He loves you; the mystery of it is that He does not command your love in return, but leaves you free, leaves you with the awesome power of choice. If He did not leave you free to choose, it would not be love. For the greatest thing about love is *to be chosen*.

Why not blame God? Once we understand the mystery of His love for us, we can't; it just isn't reasonable.

Well then, let's blame it all on the other fellow

"Oh see what he did to me!" we wail. "I was perfectly all right until *he* came along and tempted me. If he hadn't crossed my path none of this would have happened!"

"It's my parents. They're too strict. I have to sneak off to get any freedom at all and then of course I run into all these temptations that I probably wouldn't have to face if I didn't have to sneak off but I have to sneak off—"

"My parents give me too much freedom. If they didn't give me so much freedom I wouldn't be running into all these temptations."

There was a social gathering once, of Christians, that turned into one of those "truth sessions." It didn't start out to be but somehow it just happened and everybody began to talk about his problems and temptations. The variety was endless; no two people had the same kind. But they all had one common denominator. Not one of these people blamed his dilemma on himself. Every one of them was perfectly sure it had been caused by some other person or some set of circumstances beyond his control.

Because the evening had taken such a serious turn, they had a "word of prayer" before they broke up. Then everyone went home, as confused as he was before, taking his problem with him. For everyone's greatest problem was himself.

If only I hadn't met her, if only I'd gone to a different school, if only I weren't thrown in with those kids, if only he hadn't put the idea in my mind, if only they—

Come now. Didn't those people or those circumstances or that idea run into an incipient desire in you that was clamoring for attention all the time, and although your physical feet may have dragged a bit, didn't the feet of your mind "run swiftly to destruction?"

Who me?

Yes you. James says: "No, a man's temptation is due to the pull of his own inward desires, *which can* be enormously attractive" (verse 14).

The King James translation has it: "But every man is tempted, when he is drawn away of *his own lust*, and enticed."

The *Living New Testament* has it: "Temptation is the pull of man's own evil thoughts and wishes."

Ah that's the rub.

Satan does not hand you the temptation with a blueprint showing the frustration, the failure, the alienation from God, the unrealized goals, the drug rehabilitation center, the unwanted pregnancy or *whatever* the end might be. He suggests only the pleasure of the moment—and it is implicit that somehow *you* are going to get away with it and come out unscathed.

Temptation would be helpless if there were nothing in *you* to which it could appeal; it has to strike an answering chord. There is something in you that responds to the bait, and that something is your own desire. Any con man will tell you that he can't con a person whose face isn't already streaked with larceny.

Some of our desires we jolly well know about. Some of them we are not aware of, but they are there in the pit stop getting gassed and oiled, ready at the drop of a temptation to get out on the track.

That's where it starts; where does it go?

There's an old Chinese proverb that goes: "Sow a thought and reap a deed; sow a deed and reap a habit; sow a habit and reap a destiny." James puts it: "His own inward desire takes hold of him, and that produces sin. And sin in the long run means death." And in verse 16 James says: "Make no mistake about that, brothers of mine!"

It starts with a thought. And a thought toyed with long enough ultimately results in action. If you dwell on it long enough, the chances are you'll do it; it's as simple as that. And sin, as a way of life must, in the end, lead to destruction.

But times are changing

Yes. "If Booth Tarkington were to write *Seventeen* today," says a Connecticut high school English teacher, "he'd have to call it *Twelve*." You're getting older younger. And adults expect you to prepare for a job, behave like adults without being accepted as adults, do not as adults do, but as they say. To be taught the precepts of honesty and then find adults bragging about cheating on their income tax, or to be taught the precepts of good grooming and decorum and then see overweight women out shopping in stretch pants and huge hair curlers, looking like they're wired for sound, are only mild examples of what you're up against. So in frustration you turn for direction and understanding to your peers, or to the adults who are "swingers" and behave in the ways your group approves.

"I enjoy three things," said one high-schooler. "Being in a bookstore with $10 in my pocket, a rainy day at the beach, and insight in terms of finding insight in myself." Then he added, "I'm kinda hoping to make a more meaningful person out of my mother, but it's hard work."

"They're just not with it!" cried another. "Do they know what it's all about? Are they really alive?"

It's inconceivable to us that anybody anywhere ever had to face the temptations that plague us like gnats today.

Look at Romans 1:21-32:

[21]"They knew all the time that there is a God, yet they refused to acknowledge him as such, or to thank him for what he is or does. Thus they became fatuous in their argumentations, and plunged their silly minds still further into the dark. [22]Behind a façade of 'wisdom' they became just fools, [23]fools who would exchange the glory of the immortal God for an imitation image of a mortal man, or of creatures that run or fly or crawl. They gave up God: [24]and therefore God gave them up—to be the playthings of their own foul desires in dishonoring their own bodies.

[25]"These men deliberately forfeited the truth of God and accepted a lie, paying homage and giving service to the creature instead of to the Creator, who alone is worthy to be worshiped for ever and ever, amen. [26]God therefore handed them over to disgraceful passions. Their women exchanged the normal practices of sexual intercourse for something which is abnormal and unnatural. [27]Similarly the men, turning from natural intercourse with women, were swept into lustful passions for one an-

other. Men with men performed these shameful horrors, receiving, of course, in their own personalities the consequences of sexual perversity.

[28]"Moreover, since they considered themselves too high and mighty to acknowledge God, he allowed them to become the slaves of their degenerate minds, and to perform unmentionable deeds. [29]They became filled with wickedness, rottenness, greed and malice; their minds became steeped in envy, murder, quarrelsomeness, deceitfulness and spite. [30]They became whisperers-behind-doors, stabbers-in-the-back, God-haters; they overflowed with insolent pride and boastfulness, and their minds teemed with diabolical invention. They scoffed at duty to parents; [31]they mocked at learning, recognized no obligations of honor, lost all natural affection, and had no use for mercy. [32]More than this—being well aware of God's pronouncement that all who do these things deserve to die, they not only continued their own practices, but did not hesitate to give their thorough approval to others who did the same."

Well, this about covers everything, including the generation gap. People have been breaking the commandments, seeking thrills, rebelling against authority and blowing their minds since the beginning of time.

But what about us good guys?

I'm just an ordinary person, you say. I think I'm normal. I have no inclination toward mind blowing or most of the things in those verses. I have a mild case of rebellion like everybody else in the group but I expect I'll get over it. I do my thing, but it's *reasonable*. Big temptations don't come up and knock me on the head. And yet I'm getting tripped up somewhere, because I'm just not satisfied with myself as a person. The state of feeling okay with God keeps eluding me. But my goals are legitimate!

I want love—appreciation—and yes, in spite of all my talking about divorcing myself from the establishment, I want responsibility. I even want leadership—I'd like to make a try at it, to prove myself. I want to be popular. I want security. I think money is overrated but I do want security—the overall big meaning of the word. I want not to be lonely.

The name of the game

The name of the game is goals—and how you reach them. All things being equal, temptation usually presents itself in the form of a shortcut to your goal.

"I want what I want when I want it" the song goes, and "it" can mean *anything*.

When our Lord was tempted in the wilderness, Satan tempted Him in the area of His rights. Satisfying hunger, proving He is the Son of God by supernatural means, ruling the kingdoms of the earth. But if He had taken any of the shortcuts Satan proposed He would have upset the perfect plan of God and stopped short of the cross.

Shortcuts are dangerous

There was an account in a large city newspaper that was headlined:

STOLEN FUNDS FAIL TO BUY
LOVE FOR SPINSTER

"A lonely spinster who sought to buy love by stealing is in prison, and her boss may have to file for bankruptcy. Of the $109,000 she admitted taking from him, about $27,000 went to three boy-friends—described by the judge who passed sentence as 'greedy and spineless.'

"The rest of the money, the woman told a probation officer, went for an expensive apartment, extensive facial surgery, a fur coat, traveling—the works. 'The seeds of despair have done their work with efficiency, and the resultant effect seems to be this defendant's misguided attempt to buy love and affection from male companions,' the probation officer told the court. The woman told the court she gave one boyfriend $18 to 20,000, another $3 to 4,000, and yet another $3,000. 'They kept putting the bite on me,' she said. And she lamented that the first two not only accepted the money, but were unfaithful to her. The three recipients, interviewed later by police, described their benefactor as 'a soft touch.'

"The judge summed it up tersely. 'This is a very pathetic case,' he said."

Now admittedly this is such an extreme case that it borders the incredible. If it were not so pathetic it would be cornball melodrama.

But all the ingredients are here. Love was a legitimate desire. But the shortcut she took to get it boggles the mind. She might have waited for it; she might have had to face doing without it. But the end of the game she was playing makes either of those possibilities look pretty good by contrast. And the pity of it is she did not get the love she wanted after all.

Oh yes. She did not take the money all at once. She dipped into the till a little at a time, over a period of years. First there was the desire. Then there was the thought which led to the deed which led to the habit which led to a way of life which led to her ultimate destruction.

We want love and we snatch at it too soon or by the wrong rules and it turns to ashes in our greedy little fists. We want appreciation and we whine for it or demand it or try to buy it. We want responsibility and leadership and we bulldoze over others and cheat to get it. We want to be popular and we compromise our integrity to stay up there on top. We want security in its broadest sense, and we knock the props out from under every effort of God to give us *His* security. We want not to be lonely and we refuse the discipline it takes to be the sort of person others want to be around.

The goals may be legitimate all right; the snag is the shortcut.

Sex: the big hang-up

"Why," said a jaded young man wearily, "do parents have this big hang-up on sex? I'm weary of hearing about it." He was being interviewed for a national magazine. The gentleman in question was ten years old. Yes, you are getting older younger.

On the one hand, no chapter on temptation seems complete without talking about sex. On the other, it seems that everything to be said about it has been said, ad nauseum, until the subject is exhausted and so is everybody else.

"Sex is something that occurs in life. To keep it out of education, draped in curtains and labeled something different, is a gross error," said one seventeen-year-old on a panel.

"My dog having puppies was my first contact with sexuality," said another. "I had very strange notions until I was quite old—about ten years old."

"You can't talk to parents," another explained patiently, "The first thing they say is, 'What have you been doing lately,' and then they cut down your curfew. So you talk to other kids in your group and get misinformation."

"Biology," said another, who hoped to teach it some day, "is the natural place to introduce sex. But they rattle on about the human body and it's not enough to look at charts and label the parts. You have to explain; what is *desire?* And what do we do about our *feelings?*"

Another announced that lucky is the teen-ager who has a good biology teacher—"Not one who just likes plants. I learned about frogs, worms and plants. But I didn't learn anything about *myself*. From a teacher you will not hear the word 'love.'"

"We have white mice in the laboratory," said one of the teachers on the panel, "and we let the child observe copulation—and reproduction if it happens during school hours."

Ah yes. But nobody thinks to tell the children that they are *not* going to grow up to be white mice. Looking at embryos and charts and flagella and hearing about pollination will not make your sex drive go away.

One teacher on the panel mentioned that it all stemmed from "a society that forces 'restrictive cultural patterns' on children alongside public displays of topless waitresses and obscene books."

Well, yes. But why blame it all on the influences of the modern age? The no-holds-barred TV and movies and Lady Chatterley didn't start it all. From Chatterley back to Emma Bovary, back to Peter Abelard and Heloise, we have been exposed to languishing lovers, giving up all for love—illicit love. And the implication is that it is somehow sad and beautiful and very appealing. Augustine wrote that it was difficult to convince people indulging in illicit sex that they were sinning. The same is true today. "But I *love* him!" we wail. "We're so *right* for each other!" and we fail to see the difference between what sex appears to be and what it really is.

Sex does not follow a separate law aside and apart from *you*—it's a part of your total personality. It is what you are. The erotic significance, the act itself, is not the point. Sex is you. You cannot isolate it from its context, God says you cannot, it is you, it is your very character. Using it wrongly is the one sin that entrenches upon and damages your own psyche. It is the one sin you commit against yourself. "Avoid sexual looseness like the plague! Every other sin that a man commits is done outside his own body, but this is an offense against his own body" (I Corinthians 6:18).

Letting God control this area of your life is not

going to deprive you as much as you might think. God never makes us give up anything without giving us something better to replace it. Psychologists tell us that the sex drive is basically creative energy. People who have sublimated and detoured this terrific energy into other channels, are sometimes the people who are exploding with ideas or creative ability or this mysterious quality we call charisma.

In any case it's a God-given gift, and it's a pity to take anything so great and use it *against* yourself. God has much to say about illicit sex throughout the Scriptures; it can all be summed up in one word:

Don't.

Is there a way out of temptation?

Of course. God will never leave you without a way to go. "No temptation has come your way that is too hard for flesh and blood to bear. But God can be trusted not to allow you to suffer any temptation beyond your powers of endurance. He will see to it that every temptation has a way out, so that it will never be impossible for you to bear it" (I Cor. 10:13).

Our Lord said: "Watch and pray, all of you, that you may not have to face temptation. Your spirit is willing, but human nature is weak" (Matthew 26:41).

And throughout Scripture we are admonished to pray with perseverance. When the great architect Sir Christopher Wren cleared away old St. Paul's to make room for a new edifice, he had to break down the old masonry with battering rams. Day after day his workmen battered at a massive wall without seeming to make the least impression. And then one day the stubborn stone began to disintegrate. Now every blow counted. First the wall quivered, then it moved visibly, then finally it fell amid clouds of dust. But it was not really the last blows that felled it. It was a combination of *all* the blows.

If you are whamming away with no visible results, don't give up. For: "The Lord *can* rescue you and me from the temptations that surround us" (II Peter 2:9, *Living New Testament*).

And He will. He will never let you down.

The establishment may be phony; God is not

[17]"But every good endowment that we possess and every complete gift that we have received must come from above, from the Father of all lights, with whom there is never the slightest variation or shadow of inconsistency. [18]By his own wish he made us his own sons through the Word of truth, that we might be, so to speak, the first specimens of his new creation."

Through all the changes in this mad, mad, mad, mad world, God remains steadfast, unchanging, completely dependable. His gifts are good and complete. And the greatest gift He offers you is the privilege of being His child.

When God said to Adam and Eve "don't do it" and Satan said "do it" and they did it, they took themselves out of God's hands. It was their choice. So by choice they were lost. That is what being "lost" is—out of God's hands. And so everyone who was born after that was also out of God's hands.

In the course of time, when God was ready, He sent our Lord to die for this "lost" mankind, and He was punished in the place of every "lost" person. This was God's gift to every person born. Your privilege as a person is to accept this gift and thereby put yourself back into God's hands. That's what being "saved" is. That's what makes you a Christian. The terminology is unimportant, but the transaction, no matter how you word it, is the most important one you'll make in all your life.

Notice verse eighteen in *Living New Testament*. "It was a happy day for Him." For *Him?*

Yes. You are loved.

What's in it for me?

If verse 18 is true for you, there's so much in it for you, it's going to take you the rest of your life to drink it all in.

As for temptation—if you can lick that one, look at verse 12: "The man who patiently endures the temptations and trials that come to him is the truly happy man. For once his testing is complete he will receive the crown of life which the Lord has promised to all who love him."

A crown? In our Lord's time, a crown of flowers was worn at times of joy, a crown of gold was the mark of royalty, a crown of laurel leaves was the victor's crown in the games—the prize the athlete wanted above all else. You can have joy, you can be the child of the King, you can have victory, you can have the crown of abundant life in its fullest.

I've got it all — but there's one little point

Perhaps God didn't *start* it. But does He have to *allow* it? And is temptation itself sin?

Temptation isn't sin in itself; yielding to it is. And why does He allow it? Come now, if you were not tempted you would feel neglected. It is something you have to run into if you are worth your salt. The power of choice is what makes you a choice person. You wouldn't want to be a robot, would you?

Think

1. Write down the goals that are most important to you in one column. Write down what you've been doing to attain them in another. And if you've been using shortcuts, no fudging.

2. Write down some of the temptations that plague you most. What answering chord did they strike in you? Be honest with yourself.

3. Memorize I Corinthians 10:13.

3

Freedom— a thing devoutly to be wished

You'd like to be your own boss? So would we all. Dream on!

There's a story of a bee who overheard a conversation while he was dallying on a windowpane, and discovered to his dismay that he was a worker bee, born to be under authority all his life, and would never be anything else. He flew back to the hive, mad as a hornet, and got his fellow bees to rebel and fly out for themselves and establish their own colony. Well, they fell to quarreling over who would be boss, and got nowhere. In the thick of it, our little

bee left in disgust, ran into an older bee, and decided to live with *him.* "Who'll be the boss?" asked the
older bee. "Why *you*—you're the wiser." "And
who'll be the worker?" asked the older bee. "Why
me—I'm the stronger." And then he saw how things
stood. He was right back where he started from. So
they both decided to go back to the hive and let the
queen bee rule the roost, which was the way God
had planned it in the first place.

Everybody answers to some authority. Nobody is,
in the long run, his own boss.

When you stop answering to your elders, you will
start answering to a boss, who is answering to a
boss, who is answering to a boss, who is answering
to the top boss in the outfit, who is answering to his
power and money, for if he does not behave in a
certain way he will lose both. And everybody, in the
end, is answering to God.

What, then, is freedom? Or *is* there any such
thing?

The answer is yes, but the reason it eludes us is
that most of us look for it in the wrong place. We
long to be free and we seek this freedom by every
means from mild balking to open rebellion. We
think of this as self-reliance and it looks very attractive, but actually it is *dependence.* Dependence can
express itself as submission, to be sure, but it can
also express itself as negative conformity, in blind
disobedience. Actually the rebellious person is
caught in a double bind. He is in positive obedience
to the code of the "group" and in negative obedience to the pressures of the community. So he is really a pathetic sort of person, spitting into the wind

and hoping that if he keeps on doing it he'll make it go where he wants it to instead of having it fly back in his face.

And the tragedy is that while we are thus busily engaged, *real* freedom lies right within our grasp— in the Word of God!

James says, *"But the man who looks into the perfect mirror of God's law, the law of liberty ..."*

And James not only tells us where to look for this freedom we all want, but *how.* God is as anxious for you to have it as you are to get it: the instructions are explicit and detailed so you can't possibly miss out on a thing.

James 1:19-27

[19]"In view of what he has made us then, dear brothers, let every man be quick to listen but slow to use his tongue, and slow to lose his temper. [20]For man's temper is never the means of achieving God's true goodness.

[21]"Have done, then, with impurity and every other evil which touches the lives of others, and humbly accept the message that God has sown in your hearts, and which can save your souls. [22]Don't, I beg you, only hear the message, but put it into practice; otherwise you are merely deluding yourselves. [23]The man who simply hears and does nothing about it is like a man catching the reflection of his own face in a mirror. [24]He sees himself, it is true, but he goes on with whatever he was doing without the slightest recollection of what sort of person he saw in the mirror. [25]But the man who looks

into the perfect mirror of God's law, the law of liberty, and makes a habit of so doing, is not the man who sees and forgets. He puts that law into practice and he wins true happiness.

²⁶"If anyone appears to be 'religious' but cannot control his tongue, he deceives himself and we may be sure that his religion is useless. ²⁷Religion that is pure and genuine in the sight of God the Father will show itself by such things as visiting orphans and widows in their distress and keeping oneself uncontaminated by the world."

How's your listening quotient?

This is James' first concern, and it is a logical one, for if God is ever going to be able to speak to us—through His Word, through our conscience, in the classroom, in the church or wherever, it just naturally follows that we have to be good listeners. This is so obvious and elementary that it hardly seems worth mentioning, and yet the ability to listen is a talent most of us do not have. Nor want. We would rather talk than listen any day. We would deny it to the end. We ask the other fellow all about himself and, "Uh huh, uh huh, uh huh," we say and hurry on to our next question, rushing him through and then when we've gotten all that out of the way, we settle down to telling him about ourselves, saving the best part till last. We console ourselves that we've already listened to *him*, when in fact we have just got all the possible interruptions taken care of so we are free now to have the stage.

We "tune out" to avoid difficult listening. Some of us actually brag about it. "I can look a person right in the eye and never hear a word he says." In order to do this we develop the habit of "faking attention." Some of us do it well from long practice; others of us don't fool anybody.

Our reasons for doing this are legion. We are threatened or affronted, or what is being said is not pleasant or acceptable, or the person talking is a crashing bore. Whatever our reasons, we are the losers. For we miss gems of learning that may never come our way again.

Admittedly it isn't easy to listen, and the odds are against us. We have to listen to people whose thoughts are totally disorganized, to people who do not look at us while they are speaking, to people who keep saying "Do you see? Do you see?" when we not only see but are ten minutes ahead of them and have already smelled out the denouement, to people who answer our questions before we ask them ("Oh," you ask, "why do I think this? Well I'll tell you why I think this—"), to people who are saying one thing and meaning another, to people who speak in pious platitudes and vague spiritual generalities without ever getting down to cases, to people who speak so low or so rapidly that we can only guess what they're saying—

No it isn't easy. But James puts the responsibility of getting instruction from God's word *squarely on our shoulders.* [19]"In view of what he has made us then, dear brothers, let every man be quick to listen but slow to use his tongue."

He has just finished telling you that God gave you a new life through the Word of truth and offered you the choice of becoming His child, that it

42

was a happy day for Him when He did it, *that you are loved.*

You can "tune in" if you really want to

We prove this every day of our lives. And some of the things we "tune in" make us look pretty silly as Christians. Some of us run around looking for answers from people, like a lost dog at a picnic looking for a friendly person somewhere who will pat him on the head and feed him and lead him safely home. We're at the mercy of anyone who will give us an answer to our dilemma, and anyone who sounds sharp enough becomes ten feet tall and his voice is the voice of authority. We abandon ourselves to causes, to ideas, to heroes, to the latest book or program or ideology or whatever, with blind devotion. It's sharp. It's "in." It's going to solve our problem and clear our thinking and show us the way to go.

But when it comes to listening to sound instruction, we turn off our hearing aids.

Russell Conwell, founder of the great Baptist Temple in Philadelphia, became an agnostic during his first year in college. When he came home for vacation he told his father about it. They were hoeing potatoes at the time. "Russell,'" his father said, "have you forgotten the things you learned from God—have you forgotten all He has said?"

"But pa," said Russell, who was *not* slow to use his tongue, "you don't understand. You've never had an education and you just don't understand. I'm getting an education and listening to people and getting all these new ideas and concepts and it's 'in' right now to doubt that God *is*. I'm president of the Free-thinkers' Club."

He went away to war shortly after that, knowing everything there was to know. He said later in his autobiography that no young person knows more at any other time of his life than he knows during his first year at college. He's smarter than he ever was before, or than he'll ever be again. Today he would have said high school.

Anyhow Russell went away to war knowing everything there was to know except the grace of God. It took years of war and a great personal tragedy to bring him back to that. Of course his father had already told him, back there in the potato patch. But he wasn't listening.

When he got down to listening again and came to grips with the Word of God, he founded what was then the biggest fundamental Protestant church in the world, and his life shone like a beacon light and young people from all over came to hear him because now he had something worth talking about.

But can't I express my doubts?

This "listen much, speak little" is a little hard to take. I have questions. And I have doubts.

Of course.

James is talking about airing your own views at the drop of a verse without giving God a chance to speak to you. He is not talking about your honest doubts. Honest doubts are not sins. Even John Bunyan, one of the greatest Christians of all times, admitted to moods of secret unbelief. You can have questions and doubts without being torn loose from your moorings. The tide might rush in and toss you about a bit. And you might get seasick but you won't sink.

In Bunyan's *Pilgrim's Progress*, poor Mr. Ready-to-Halt was so hung up on doubts that he went all the way to the Celestial City on crutches. He got there all right, but he missed most of the joy on the way.

Do you have a short fuse?

Of course most of us would rather couch it in more acceptable terminology. "I'm high-strung" we say, ("Like a thoroughbred," we think). It makes us feel more comfortable. Anything is better than coming right out and admitting that we have a short fuse, that we explode at the drop of a hint, or that we are opinionated or dogmatic or domineering or any of those boring things that make us miserable people to be around.

Some of us are even secretly proud of having a short fuse. It's an effective weapon in getting our own way. Everyone treads carefully in our presence and we bulldoze through life, proud of every inch of ground we gain and mistaking other peoples' acquiescence for approval, never realizing that they would rather tread carefully than be bored stiff with another replay of our nasty temper. Or that if they weren't good Christians they would probably never put up with us in the first place.

James goes on. Let's take verses 19 and 20 all together: "In view of what he has made us then, dear brothers, let every man be quick to listen but slow to use his tongue, and slow to lose his temper. For man's temper is never the means of achieving God's true goodness."

If you do have a short fuse, the problem is that while you are busy bulldozing or arguing when you should be listening, you miss golden opportunities for instruction, for growth, for development into the person God meant you to be. And the tragedy is that the only person you are really short-changing is yourself.

James is not saying you may never get angry. Our Lord was angry upon occasion. And Paul tells us to "be angry and sin not." James is merely saying "watch it." Be as slow to anger as you are quick to listen.

We feel the pinch

We become angry and argue over the Word of God because it hits a sore spot somewhere; it threatens to infringe upon our right to ourselves. It hits us in an area where we're not ready to give in yet. Or it exposes a weakness in us that we've been touting as a virtue.

There's a story about a woman, many years ago, who shouted "Amen!" in church every time the preacher admonished against a vice. Then he mentioned snuff, and she was heard to mutter, "Now he's messing around." He had intruded in her domain and she felt the pinch.

We become angry with people because we feel threatened; they are going to do us in if we don't rear up and fight. Or we become angry with someone because we were leaning on him and he let us down, when we had no business to be leaning on him in the first place. Or we become angry with adults because we suspect they are phony, without stopping to think that if we are sharp enough to suspect they are phony we should be mature enough to forgive them. Or we become angry over side issues, or at the wrong person or for the wrong reason. Sinful anger is always associated with confusion; the real issue is always clouded.

Don't take anger lightly: it's dynamite

This sad little filler was in the Los Angeles Times: "Paragraph for people who Blow-Their-Tops and lose their tempers. Happened in the upper 50's on the East Side the other night . . . A man of about 55 and his wife quarreled with another driver . . . Over parking space . . . Bystanders convinced the police that the other driver didn't strike a blow . . . that the 55-year-older punched the other driver twice . . . He allegedly slugged his wife twice when she urged him to calm down . . . Then he walked ten steps and dropped dead."

If this were a contrived illustration it would be unbelievable and even corny. But it really happened. Over a parking space.

This poor wretch did not suddenly form the habit of becoming this angry; he had made anger a habit all his life until all the little angers grew and grew and enslaved him—and in the end, did him in.

What to do with the culprit?

Don't. Don't put it in the deepfreeze. You won't get rid of it that way. It will fester and come out in some other way. You're not quite old enough to have it come out in high blood pressure or ulcers, but it will trip you up in some way; it's up to no good.

The worst way to deal with anger is to pretend to yourself that you're not angry. Or to call it righteous indignation when it isn't. Remember, whether you clench your fists and shout, speak in low measured tones, or just sigh a superior sigh and go off and sulk in martyrlike silence—it is still anger.

Do. Make an honest attempt to resolve it. The dictionary tells us that "resolve" means to fix or settle by deliberate choice and will; to cause to disintegrate, to reduce by mental analysis, deal with, solve, etc.

The Holy Spirit of God is the only one who can clear away the confusion in your own heart. After you've gone to God with it, you might try "talking it out" with whoever. But after you've gone to God, there may not be anything left to "talk out"; the whole dreary mess may have disintegrated.

Out, out, out!

James goes on: "Have done, then, with impurity and every other evil which touches the lives of others."

He's talking about real housecleaning.

Off with it. It means "off with it" as if you were stripping off filthy clothes or washing filth off from your body.

Away with it. It means "away with it" as if you were clearing away underbrush and weeds and whatever stops the crop from growing.

Out with it. It means "out with it," a derivative from the word meaning to clean wax from your ear, which is a pretty sly inference when you stop to think about it.

There's the old joke that went around among the small fry (or it should have been confined to the small fry):

"You've got a carrot in your ear."

"What?"

"You've got a carrot in your ear!"

"*What?*"

"You've got a carrot in your ear!!!"

"I CAN'T HEAR YOU—I'VE GOT A CARROT IN MY EAR!!!"

It's appallingly corny, the kind of joke eight-year-olds laugh at, but in some ridiculous way it fits here. God is trying to tell you you have sin in your life and you can't hear Him because you have sin in your life.

Let's check the list out so far

James is telling us that real freedom comes from obedience to the Word of God. And so far he has said in effect: be quick to listen, slow to speak, slow to anger—diligent about getting rid of the weeds or wax or whatever is hindering you in your life. Even crud is in the dictionary now, and it's a repulsive word—but so is sin.

And then he tells us to "humbly accept the message that God has sown in your hearts, and which can save your souls."

I've got my instructions: now what?

Well don't put them away for safekeeping, like a bride puts away her silverware to tarnish.

You can't get nourishment by staring at a recipe. Or build a boat by staring at the instructions. Or pass an exam by staring at the questions. The TWA commercial would not impress us if all those gourmet meals were served on the ground. It's the "Up, up and AWAY!" that gets us.

James 1:22-27

[22]"Don't, I beg you, only hear the message, but put it into practice; otherwise you are merely deluding yourselves. [23]The man who simply hears and does nothing about it is like a man catching the reflection of his own face in a mirror. [24]He sees himself, it is true, but he goes on with whatever he was doing without the slightest recollection of what sort of person he saw in the mirror. [25]But the man who looks into the perfect mirror of God's law, the law of liberty, and makes a habit of so doing, is not the

man who sees and forgets. He puts that law into practice and he wins true happiness.

[26]"If anyone appears to be 'religious' but cannot control his tongue, he deceives himself and we may be sure that his religion is useless. [27]"Religion that is pure and genuine in the sight of God the Father will show itself by such things as visiting orphans and widows in their distress and keeping oneself uncontaminated by the world."

Go, go, go!

We get right down to cases here; there's no build-up to cushion the blow. We're told right off to get up and get going: "Don't, I beg you, only hear the message, but put it into practice; otherwise you are merely deluding yourselves."

Don't be the chap who goes to church and listens to the sermon and goes to youth meetings and takes part in the buzz session and goes to Sunday School and listens to the teaching—

—and folds up his halo and goes away, happy

and content that he has done *his* Christian bit—let the other fellow beware!

Mirror mirror on the wall

In verses 23 and 24 James gives a graphic picture of the chap who listens and doesn't *do*: "The man who simply hears and does nothing about it is like a man catching the reflection of his own face in a mirror. He sees himself, it is true, but he goes on with whatever he was doing without the slightest recollection of what sort of person he saw in the mirror."

In those days mirrors were made of polished metal and in these days they are made of plate glass and really give us the works (especially those ghastly contraptions that have a magnifying mirror on one side) but the analogy is still the same. We see our imperfections. But in either case, we go away, forgetting what we look like. The fact that we (the girls get ribbed for it but the boys do it too) are periodically running off to a mirror to check up on our appearance proves it. We can't remember what we looked like an hour ago.

Like a mirror, the Word of God gives us a reflection of ourselves.

There's the story of the elderly gentleman who was very nearsighted—(stories like these are always fun to tell about *other* people)—and who prided himself on his ability as an art critic.

Well, it seems that one day this gentleman and his wife were accompanying some friends through a large art gallery, and he took it upon himself to play guide and display his real or fancied knowledge to his friends. Unfortunately he'd left his glasses home, but this did not deter him. He stood before one large frame and began to expound. "In the first place," said he, "the frame is altogether out of keeping with the subject—"

His wife, who was standing in the back of the group, paled visibly.

"And as for the subject itself," he spouted (it was a man), "it is altogether too homely, in fact, too ugly, ever to make a good picture."

"Pssst—" said his wife as she edged her way to the front.

"It's a great mistake for any artist to choose so homely a subject for a picture if he expects it to be a masterpiece—"

"Psssst," said his wife again, frantic now.

"Or, if he does, the face should at least have some character."

"Pssst," said his wife, who was up to the front by now. "You are looking in a mirror."

The Word of God is like a mirror that gives us a reflection of ourselves—and we don't always like what we see.

Can this be me? Auuugggghhhh?!

Every morning the blow is just as great. Can this puffy-eyed bedraggled wreck of humanity be I? That first look in the mirror that shows us how we look (ugh) *before we hide our imperfections*, takes a lot of courage. Our "morning face" is one we'd just as soon forget.

The Word of God shows us what we are without our pretenses—without our camouflage. And James is talking about the person who sees the things that

Auuugggghhhh!

are wrong in his life and goes away and soon forgets.

Look again

"But," says James in verse 25, "the man who looks into the perfect mirror of God's law, the law of liberty, and makes a habit of so doing, is not the man who sees and forgets. He puts that law into practice and he wins true happiness."

Ah now, here James means business. In verse 24 he was talking about a hasty glance and away we go, but here, the verb he uses means bending over a mirror, peering intently into it, examining what it reveals, with great care.

"But who wants to look again?" you say, "if all I can see is my weaknesses and faults and ugliness? I don't *like* my 'morning face.' It seems to me I'd be happier if I read some modern psychology—some do-it-yourself—something that tells me how nice I am. I *like* myself with the camouflage, and I want it to stay that way."

But wait.

"I've got enough problems. Look at myself as I really am? Who needs it?"

Are you still muttering? Read on.

There's a wonderful story about a couple of Pilgrims who were on their way to the Celestial City (it's Bunyan's *Pilgrim's Progress* again). And they got up in some mountains and ran into some Shepherds. And the Shepherds gave them a beautiful looking glass. "Now the glass was one in a thousand," writes Bunyan. "It would reflect a man, one way, with his own features exactly; *but turn it another way,* and it would show the very face of the Prince of pilgrims Himself. Yea, I have talked with those who can tell, and they've said they have seen the very crown of thorns upon His head by looking into this glass; they've seen also the holes in His hands, in His feet, and His side. Yea, such an excellency is there in this glass, that it will show Him to one, *if he has a mind to see Him. . . ."*

And keep looking. . .

Your Lord is in that mirror, "if you have a mind to see Him." The do-it-yourself psychology book will tell you to "know" yourself and to "adjust to yourself," and to "accept yourself," and to "forgive yourself." But in the Word of God you can know yourself and adjust to yourself with the enlightenment of the Holy Spirit, and accept yourself because *God* has accepted you and forgive yourself because *He* has forgiven you. And the more you look the more clearly you'll see Him and what He has done for you, and still wants to do.

Did James say law? Is this a snag?

Yes James said law and no it isn't a snag. He said, "But the man who looks into the perfect mirror of God's law, the law of liberty. . . ." *Living New Testament* puts it: "But if anyone keeps looking steadily into God's law for free men. . . ."

The Christian law is the law of *liberty*, and it is

only in the keeping of it that you can *find* true liberty. Are you a slave to anger? Your emotions? Your desires? What is your hang-up? Whatever it is, if you're obeying it, you're a slave to it. It's only when you accept the will of God and obey the law of God that you are really free—free to be the terrific person you want to be!

What's this?

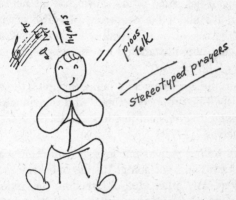

In the last two verses of this chapter, James brings us up with a jolt: "If anyone appears to be 'religious' but cannot control his tongue, he deceives himself and we may be sure that his religion is useless. Religion that is pure and genuine in the sight of God the Father will show itself by such things as visiting orphans and widows in their distress and keeping oneself uncontaminated by the world."

What he's talking about seems pretty obvious at a glance, but what is he *really* talking about? The King James translation says, "If any man among you seem to be religious—" —and the meaning of the word "religious" means the *outward expression* of it. He's talking about worship services and prayer meetings and such. He's not against them. He's merely saying that they cannot take the place of *service*. And he's warning that they *can* degenerate into mere formalities that get emptier and emptier as we say and do the same things over and over again.

Bunyan has some biting satire that fits here very nicely; it's about his character, Mr. Talkative. He was "the son of one Saywell who dwelt in Prating Row, and notwithstanding his fine tongue, he is but a sorry fellow."

So in the last two verses James dropping the same bombshell he dropped before: "And remember, it is a message to *obey*, not just to listen to. So don't fool yourselves" (*LNT*).

He's telling you to put legs on your Christianity and get up and get going! It's the only way to true freedom. Any other kind of "freedom" or "independence" or whatever you want to call it, is a snare and a delusion.

Think

Liberty—use it! "And ye shall know the truth, and the truth shall make you free" (John 8:32, KJV).

"For the law of the Spirit of life in Christ Jesus hath made me free from the law of sin and death" (Romans 8:2, KJV).

"Now the Lord is that Spirit: and where the

Spirit of the Lord is, there is liberty" (II Corinthians 3:17, KJV).

Don't abuse it! "For, brethren, ye have been called unto liberty; only use not liberty for an occasion to the flesh, but by love serve one another" (Galatians 5:13, KJV).

"As free, and not using your liberty for a cloke of maliciousness, but as the servants of God" (I Peter 2:16, KJV).

4

What kind
of a snob are you?

All right—I'm ready to go!

You have your instructions from God Himself—James calls Him "the Lord of Glory."

You've seen yourself, lost without Christ, a complete person only in Him, and you're in earnest about this business of being a Christian. It's the greatest thing that has ever happened to you. As one chap said at a high school conference—"It's so absolutely out of sight I just can't believe it."

But what's this?

People? Well, yes. It isn't *too* much of a jolt. You knew you were going to have to deal with people. You're not like the missionary who wrote home, "The work here is great—except for those natives." You're not so much up in the clouds that you are no good for earth. You *like* people, really.

But James says: "Don't ever attempt, my brothers, to combine snobbery with faith in our glorious Lord Jesus Christ!"

Well of course you're selective. Any discriminating person is. You have a right to select your own friends. Is James against friendship?

Friendship is good

Friendship is good and right and proper; each person has a right to select his personal friends. We are drawn to certain people because we can "communicate" with them. A communicating hallway connects two rooms, so to say "We really connected!" is not as slangy as it might seem. Friends "connect" because they enjoy the same things, have things in common, like to talk to each other—just plain *like* each other. Friendship is something to thank God for and cherish. Then what is James talking about?

Are you a snob?

James is talking about more than just being drawn to certain people. Let's have it all; then we'll take it a bit at a time:

James 2:1-13

[1]"Don't ever attempt, my brothers, to combine snobbery with faith in our glorious Lord Jesus Christ! [2]Suppose one man comes into your meeting well dressed and with a gold ring on his finger, and another man, obviously poor, arrives in shabby clothes. [3]If you pay special attention to the well dressed man by saying, 'Please sit here—it's an excellent seat,' and say to the poor man, 'You stand over there, please, or if you must sit, sit on the floor,' [4]doesn't that prove that you are making class distinctions in your mind, and setting yourselves up to assess a man's quality?—a very bad thing. [5]For do notice, my brothers, that God chose poor men, whose only wealth was their faith, and made them heirs to the kingdom promised to those who love him. [6]And if you behave as I have suggested, it is

the poor man that you are insulting. Look around you. Isn't it the rich who are always trying to 'boss' you? Isn't it the rich who drag you into litigation? 'Isn't it usually the rich who blaspheme the glorious name by which you are known?

⁸"If you obey the royal law, expressed by the scripture. 'Thou shalt love thy neighbor as thyself', all is well. ⁹But once you allow any invidious distinctions to creep in, you are sinning; you have broken God's law. ¹⁰Remember that a man who keeps the whole Law but for a single exception is none the less a law-breaker. ¹¹The one who said, 'Thou shalt not commit adultery,' also said, 'Thou shalt do no murder.' If you were to keep clear of adultery but were to murder a man you would have become a breaker of God's whole Law.

¹²"Anyway, you should speak and act as men who will be judged by the law of freedom. ¹³The man who makes no allowances for others will find none made for him. It is still true that 'mercy smiles in the face of judgment.'"

"But James was talking about the early church!"

Well this *is* a dramatic vignette of first century church life. In those days the rich were very very rich and had all the rights and the poor were very poor and had *no* rights.

In verses 6 and 7 the picture is a grim one, in the light of those times. Moneylending was a racket and the interest was practically robbery. And they had a custom of "summary arrest," which simply meant that if a rich creditor met a poor debtor on the street, he could grab the unfortunate fellow by the scruff of the neck and drag him off to the law courts. So the poor were in awe of the rich—and then along came our Lord and turned the whole social status quo askew!

Just imagine! Into the church service comes a man of great wealth, clothed in silken robes, his fingers beringed. (In those days the very rich wore several rings on every finger except the middle finger—and even *hired* rings to wear when they wanted to make an impression.) And he finds himself seated next to a slave—or worse still, a slave might even be in charge of the service. Naturally, everyone scurries about to seat the wealthy tycoon properly; old habits are hard to discard, and old customs are hard to upset. *But*:

"God chose poor men, whose only *wealth was their faith*," says James in verse 5. So *everybody* who has Christ is rich; Christianity has reduced all of us to one common denominator!

But wait. Something's wrong here. We don't want to go down without a try. "Wait a *minute!*" we wail, "the law tells me to love my neighbor as myself— it's my duty to welcome the rich guy!" And James knocks that one down in verses 8 and 9.

"Yes indeed," he says, "if you are welcoming him because you love him as you do yourself and you are giving him the same kind of welcome you would like to receive—that is fine. But if the special welcome is because he is rich—that is *not* so fine. In fact it is sin." James is not talking about being nice to the rich; he is talking about fawning over them and truckling to them *because* they are rich.

"Well that lets me out!"

"If there's one thing I'm *not* a snob about, it's money," you say. "I have it and I don't look down on people who don't." Or, "I don't have it and I don't envy people who do. Young people don't care about money anymore. Our thing is insight and unphoniness and love."

Yes. If there's one all-encompassing truth about young people today it is that they are making an unprecedented attempt to be honest. And if there's one all-encompassing truth about snobbery it is that there is more than one way to be a snob.

What kind of a snob are you?

It really isn't a question of whether or not we are snobs, but rather what kind of snobs we *are*. Consciously or unconsciously, in one way or another, we draw a little circle:

And anyone or anything outside that circle:

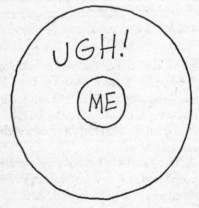

Remember Jonah? In all the wrangling over that fish, the main point of the story is often lost—namely, how did Jonah get into such a mess? What was he doing in the fish in the first place?

Jonah was the kind of a man who prays the prayer, "Lord send a revival and let it begin in me"

—which is a pretty safe prayer, nice and general, skirting neatly around details and leaving us feeling mighty spiritual. He was all out for God.

But then it came down to *specifics*. "Jonah," said God, "get thee up and go to Nineveh and tell them to repent, or I shall destroy them."

Nineveh? Pagans! Political enemies! Never!

And Jonah picked up his money pouch and went to the seaport and bought a ticket for Tarshish—which was in the opposite direction.

And even after his soul-shaking experience and his narrow escape from death—when he finally *did* go to Nineveh and preach to them and they *did* repent—he sat outside the city walls and sulked!

Jonah was a narrow-minded patriot who feared his political enemies, and it never entered his thinking that God might love *them*.

In Jonah's outer circle the main thing that obsessed him was an enemy country. How about us?

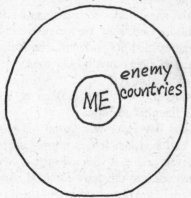

Remember Cornelius and Peter? (Acts 10, 11, *LNT*.) Cornelius was a godly man, deeply reverent, and he gave generously to charity and was a man of prayer. But he was a *Roman*. Back in those days Christianity was only for the Jews—it had started with the Jews and some of them acted as if they had invented it. Back in those days many a good Christian Jew might say, "I have nothing against the Romans. Some of my best friends are Romans," but that's as far as he would go. Romans were definitely in the outer circle.

So as devout a man as Cornelius was, he still had the best to learn. He still had to learn about CHRIST. But he was in the outer circle and naturally no one had witnessed to him.

Well, one day Cornelius was praying and he suddenly had a vision—and in this vision he saw an angel of God coming toward him. "Cornelius!" the angel said.

Cornelius stared at him in terror. "What do you want?" he said.

And the angel said, "Your prayers have not gone unnoticed by God. Now send some men to Joppa to find a man named Simon Peter, who is staying with Simon the tanner, down by the shore, and ask him to come and visit you."

Cornelius promptly called three of his servants and sent them off to Joppa.

The next day Peter was up on *his* roof praying and *he* had a vision. It was a great sheet lowered from heaven, and in it were all sorts of animals that were forbidden to the Jews for food. And a voice said to him, "Go kill and eat any of them you wish."

Peter was scandalized!

"*Never*, Lord," he said. "I've never in my life

eaten such creatures—it's forbidden by our Jewish laws."

"Don't contradict God!" said the voice. "If He says something is kosher, it's kosher!"

This vision was repeated three times; then the sheet was pulled up again to heaven. Peter was thoroughly mystified. What did it mean? What on earth was he supposed to do?

And at that moment, the two servants Cornelius had sent, knocked at the gate.

"Three men have come to see you," said the voice to Peter. "Go meet them and do as they ask. All is well; I have sent them."

So Peter went down and said, "I'm the man you're looking for. What do you want?" And when they told him what they wanted, Peter stirred himself and got out of his little inner circle and went with them.

And when he got to that outer circle he found Cornelius and all his relatives and friends waiting anxiously to hear what God wanted them to know.

At this moment Peter stopped being a snob. "I see very clearly," he said, "that the Jews are not God's only favorites!" And he began to witness. "I'm sure you have heard the Good News . . ." and "You no doubt know that Jesus . . ." and "All the prophets have written about Him . . ." and "Everyone who believes in Him will have their sins forgiven through His name. . . ." And he talked and talked until by the Holy Spirit they were talked right into the kingdom of God!

And when Peter got back to his friends, he had some explaining to do. "You fellowshiped with those Romans and even ate with them!" they roared.

And Peter told them the whole story and ended with, "And since it was *God* who gave them the same gift He gave us, who was I to argue?"

Who indeed.

Until God spoke to him, Peter's hang-up in his outer circle was other religions. How about us?

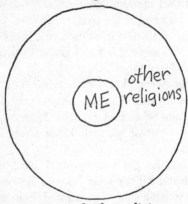

But other countries and other religions are only the beginning.

Rich man, poor man, beggar man, thief

. . . Doctor, Lawyer, Merchant, Chief, as the old game goes. The things we can be snobs about would fill a book. Education—("Did you know he comes from one of those small country colleges?") Family background—("She's pulled herself up by the bootstraps, but, my dear, you should see her *family—*") Intellect—("He's a dud in any intelligent conversation—he's just not quite bright.") Personality—("I can hardly stand her—she's a bore.")

Even sins! ("I don't know how she *ever* could have done such a thing. I would never trip over *that* temptation!"*)

And so the outer circle fills up:

The old reverse-angle

Are you one of those in the outer circle? It can work both ways.

*No, you would trip over another temptation *she* wouldn't trip over. Or you would condone a sin in someone else that might not seem as bad. There is no such thing as a respectable sin.

73

You can be a snob about *snobs*, either banded together in a group, or you can carry on a campaign all by yourself.

Let's call it what it is

James tells us in verse 9 that you are sinning. "But it's such a little one," you say. "I don't commit any of the big ones; can't I have my little quirks?"

No, and it isn't a quirk. It is sin. He goes on to say:

[10]"Remember that a man who keeps the whole Law but for a single exception is none the less a law-breaker. [11]The one who said 'Thou shalt not commit adultery,' also said, 'Thou shalt do no murder.' If you were to keep clear of adultery but were to murder a man you would have become a breaker of God's whole Law."

He is saying in effect that the God who says you must not commit adultery also said you must not be a snob.

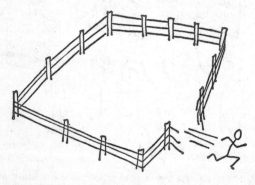

The point is, it doesn't matter *where* you broke

out of the fence or *how* you broke out, but that you did!

¹²"Anyway, you should speak and act as men who will be judged by the law of freedom. ¹³The man who makes no allowances for others will find none made for him."

There is no room for two circles

The Lord said,
"Come unto Me,
all ye that labor and
are heavy laden..."
Matt 11:28

Our Lord was available to *everybody*. He was a friend to the rich like Joseph of Arimathaea (John 19:38). He commended the poor woman who gave two mites into the Temple treasury (Luke 21:2,3). He went to the home of a Pharisee (Luke 7:36). He ate with a hated publican, Zacchaeus (Luke 19:5). He healed the servant of a Roman centurion (Luke 7:2,10). He took time out to speak to a woman of Samaria and bring her *and her whole village* to Himself (John 4).

In Bunyan's *Pilgrim's Progress*, when the Pilgrims got to the gate of the Celestial City, they "turned in, each man, his certificate, which they had received in the beginning." The certificates were carried to the king, who read them and said, "Open the gate, that they may enter in."

What was on the certificates? Letters of recommendation? Proof of superior educations? Proof of wealth? Proof of poverty? Proof of race? A membership card in a minority group?

No—proof of their salvation. The certificates had been given to them the moment they accepted Christ as Saviour, became children of God, and were made new creatures in Christ Jesus.

Don't be a snob. Don't even be a snob *about* snobs. It doesn't pay.

Read the rest of verse 13: "It is still true that 'mercy smiles in the face of judgment.'"

Think

1. Are you in a clique?* Make a list of the reasons why. Is it worth it? How can you (or your clique)

*A clique is where the "popular" people congregate to reassure each other that they really are.

make your church a friendlier place to be in? (If you and your clique really work this one out, the clique will be 'out" too!)

2. Make a list of the things you feel you are snobbish about. Stare at it for awhile. Don't you feel silly?

5
Don't just stand there—
do something

John Bunyan was a photographer before photography was invented. With exquisite sarcasm and not without humor, he draws the character of Mr. Talkative: "He talks of prayer, of repentance, of the new birth, and of faith; but he knows but only to *talk* of them. I have been in his family, and his house is as empty of religion as the white of an egg is of flavor." And with that graphic picture, Mr. Talkative goes quietly down the drain; we can only laugh at him.

The tongue in your head and the tongues in your shoes

You have one tongue in your head and two tongues in your shoes, and no matter what the tongue in your head is saying, the tongues in your shoes tell what you are *doing* and where you are *going*. And the awful truth is that the tongues in your *shoes* have the last word.

The great (and late) Dr. Alfred Adler built the approach to his theory of "individual psychology" on the admonition: "Trust only movement." He contended that life happens at the level of *actions*, not *words*. What we say is neither here nor there unless it is in agreement with our actions. We are what we *do!* And what we *do* is the real answer to what we mean and intend.

Faith + nothing = nothing

But before Dr. Adler built his famous approach to his famous theory, a greater-than-he (namely, James) led by the Holy Spirit of God, said in effect, the same thing:

James 2:14-26

[14]"Now what use is it, my brothers, for a man to say he 'has faith' if his actions do not correspond with it? Could that sort of faith save anyone's soul? [15]If a fellow man or woman has no clothes to wear and nothing to eat, [16]and one of you say, 'Good luck to you, I hope you'll keep warm and find enough to eat,' and yet give them nothing to meet their physical needs, what on earth is the good of that? [17]Yet that is exactly what a bare faith without a corresponding life is like—useless and dead. [18]If we only 'have faith' man could easily challenge us by saying: 'You say that you have faith and I have merely good actions. Well, all you can do is to show me a faith without corresponding actions, but I can show you by my actions that I have faith as well.'

[19]"To the man who thinks that faith by itself is enough I feel inclined to say, 'So you believe that there is one God? That's fine. So do all the devils in hell, and shudder in terror!' [20]For, my dear short-sighted man, can't you see far enough to realize that faith without the right actions is dead and useless? [21]Think of Abraham, our ancestor. Wasn't it his action which really justified him in God's sight when his faith led him to offer his son Isaac on the altar? [22]Can't you see that his faith and his actions

82

were, so to speak, partners—that his faith was implemented by his deed? ²³That is what the scripture means when it says: And Abraham believed God, And it was reckoned unto him for righteousness; And he was called the friend of God. ²⁴A man is justified before God by what he does as well as by what he believes. ²⁵Rahab, who was a prostitute and a foreigner, has been quoted as an example of faith, yet surely it was her action that pleased God, when she welcomed Joshua's reconnoitering party and sent them safely back by a different route.

²⁶"Yes, faith without action is as dead as a body without a soul."

"That's not the way I heard it"

"What's this?" you say. "Isn't James getting a bit high-handed here? I was with him up to this point, but now he's flying right in the teeth of all my concepts. I thought I was saved by *faith*—faith plus nothing."

You are right. You *are* saved by faith plus nothing. It is the grace of God, and nothing you could possibly do could merit it. "Therefore, we conclude that a man is justified by faith without the deeds of the law" (Romans 3:28, KJV) says Paul, and again he says, "A man is not justified by the works of the law, but by the faith of Jesus Christ . . . *for by the works of the law shall no flesh be justified*" (Galatians 2:16) and *again* he says, "Believe on the Lord Jesus Christ and thou shalt be saved" (Acts 16:31, KJV). It couldn't be plainer.

But . . .

Paul is talking about when you were over here . . .

. . . and God called you out of the darkness . . .

. . . into His wonderful light (I Peter 2:9, *Living New Testament*).

84

You got here by faith plus nothing. It was the grace of God.

But now that you *have* accepted your Lord by faith, and stepped from darkness into light—now that you *are* here, the ground rules are different. To take this step and then do nothing, makes about as much sense as whamming a ball over the back fence for a homer and then just standing there on home plate.

Now of course this business of "works" is an inclination you just don't come by naturally. To begin with, you were probably born lazy (most of us are) and our culture is programmed to see that you stay this way. It is a national habit to do more and more for children and expect less and less of them. Even the toothpaste commercial mother is considered perfectly normal when she can't get the child to brush his teeth unless she rides on his back. And in the commercial where all the kids in the family go off in different directions and either skip their lunches or buy banana splits with their lunch money, the mother looks at us viewers and wails, "What's a mother to do?"

Then suddenly, when you are in your teens, adults begin to notice that you're not doing what you haven't been doing all along, and "Oh!" they say and "Ah!" and "Why doesn't he act more mature and accept his responsibilities!" From a human standpoint, considering your inside proclivities and outside influences, you have absolutely nothing going for you.

This is a new you

But by the grace of God, this is a new you! You have stepped from darkness into light by faith—and you have accepted Christ, not only into your mind, but into every part of your life. Now it's time for action.

Don't just stand there—do something

Our Lord Himself taught that men should so live that the world might see their good works. "Don't hide your light!" He said. "Let it shine for all; let your good deeds glow for all to see, so that they will praise your heavenly Father" (Matthew 5:16, LNT). He had something to say about the "talkers" too. "Not all who talk like godly people are," He said. "They may refer to Me as 'Lord,' but still won't get to heaven" (Matthew 7:21, LNT). What He is saying is that talking can never take the place of doing the will of God.

Now that you are a Christian, Paul has a few things to say too, and he doesn't mince words. "It is to God alone that we have to answer for our actions" he says in Romans 14:12. "For every one of us will have to stand without pretense before Christ our judge," he says in II Corinthians 5:10. "And we shall be rewarded for what we did when we lived in our bodies, whether it was good or bad." In Ephesians 2:9,10 he tells us, "No one can pride himself upon earning the love of God. The fact is that what we are we owe to the hand of God upon us. For we are his workmanship, created in Christ Jesus *to do those good deeds which God planned for us to do.*"

James says: [14]"Now what use is it, my brothers, for a man to say he 'has faith' if his actions do not correspond with it? Could that sort of faith save anyone's soul? [15]If a fellow man or woman has no clothes to wear and nothing to eat, [16]and one of you say, 'Good luck to you, I hope you'll keep warm and find enough to eat,' and yet give them nothing to meet their physical needs, what on earth is the good of that? [17]Yet that is exactly what a bare faith without a corresponding life is like—useless and dead."

"Faith will out"

What are you doing about your faith? If it's a *living* faith it will have to bust out somewhere. It won't stay hidden.

Felipe Alou, veteran major leaguer got a telegram from an old friend back in the Dominican Republic, congratulating him on his first game with the Giants. "Congratulations, old friend," it went, "I have prayed for your success. But, remember, even a big-league ballplayer needs Christ. You'll find that baseball is not everything. 'Be not wise in thine own eyes: fear the Lord.'" Felipe's eyes brimmed with tears as he realized the telegram must have cost his friend half a week's wages. And he began to read the Bible this very friend had given him at the airport two and a half years before.* Felipe Alou came to know Christ because his friend had faith and he was *proving* it.

In the diary of lovely Carlie Lane ("I Walk a Joy-

*Hefley, Jim. "The Bravest Brave," *Campus Life*, April 1966, p. 21. (adapted) ful Road"—diary of a brand-new Christian)* the first entry starts with four simple words: "I accepted Christ tonight."

And the whole thing could have stopped right there, but Carlie's faith was for real. A few entries later: "Tonight I went to visit a needy family in our congregation, with my few gifts . . . Nothing in the world could match the wonderful Christmas feeling I got in that house . . . My heart just felt as if it would burst when I walked down those steps and back to the car . . . I am grateful to God for his wonderful gift to me."*

You can't be saved by works. But you can't be saved without *producing* works, any more than you can fall in love without wanting to please your loved one.

You're apt to get an argument

If you have "only faith," (without works, that is). And James tells us what that argument might be:

*Lane, Carlie. "I Walk a Joyful Road," *Campus Life*, January 1968, pp. 17,18.

[26]"If we only 'have faith' man could easily challenge us by saying: 'You say that you have faith and I have merely good actions. Well, all you can do is to show me a faith without corresponding actions, but I can show you by my actions that I have faith as well.'"

It's an excellent argument, and if your faith *is* empty, it's an argument to stop you cold! Any "do-gooder" can come along and make mince-meat out of your pious talk.

The point is, no one can set himself up, as it were, as a specialist in FAITH ONLY:

or as a specialist in GOOD DEEDS ONLY:

—and then sit down and rock and think that's all there is to it.

That is *not* "all there is to it"—in *either* case. The good deeds are empty without the saving faith in Jesus Christ. And a mere *profession* of faith ("I raised my hand and went to the altar; so what else is new?") is empty without *proving* it by good works.

What else is new?

There is a glorious "new" for you! You were saved unto "good works." "What we are we owe to the hand of God upon us. . . . We are . . . created in Christ Jesus to do those good deeds which God planned for us to do" (Ephesians 2:10). And "work *out*" what He has worked *in* you. (See Philippians 2:12,13.)

But James goes on, like a lawyer stalking his prey; he is not going to let you off.

Do you have a "pie in the sky" God?

"Well, I believe there must be something or somebody up there ruling the cosmos, you know—the 'Man Upstairs' sort of thing—you know, 'Somebody up there likes me—'"

And you reminisce fondly over your favorite baseball player when he dies —"Well, he's gone to that baseball diamond in the sky, to be with that great coach who watches over all baseball players—"

Or are you a creed-carrier?

Are you depending on your church creed or on liturgy?

"I believe in one God and I say it and say it and *say* it—every Sunday." And you carry your "creed" like a credit card, and your credit card says "I'm a Christian—and you'd better believe it!"

"Humbug!" roars James. He will have none of it. It won't do. *Neither* will do. He says: [14]"To the man who thinks that faith by itself is enough I feel in-

91

clined to say, 'So you believe that there is one God? That's fine. So do all the devils in hell, and shudder in terror!' For, my dear shortsighted man, can't you see far enough to realize that faith without the right actions is dead and useless?"

The word literally means "empty-headed" man. James is pulling no punches!

And now (verses 21-25) he neatly reduces everyone to one common denominator by using as examples of faith, two people who are poles apart in backgrounds, qualifications and temperament. It would be difficult to find two people more unlike.

The first one is Abraham—patriarch, nobleman, rich and respected. Abraham, in response to God's command, offered up his son Isaac on an altar. Now Abraham's *faith* had already been declared when he left his country and went to parts unknown, thirty years before, just because he *believed God*. Offering Isaac was a *result* of that faith.

The other one is Rahab—a Gentile, a woman, a prostitute, a nobody. Rahab hid two Israelite spies and sneaked them out of town to safety by letting them down the wall from her window. But Rahab's *faith* had already been declared when she first let those spies into her house and declared to them, "I know that the Lord your God is God in heaven above, and in earth beneath" (Joshua 2:11). Smuggling them out and saving their lives was a *result* of that faith.

No exceptions to the rule

Now James could have gone on and filled a book with examples, but by taking those two extremes he is telling us that nobody is exempt. "Don't just stand there—do something!" applies to all of us.

But doesn't God know my faith already?

Of course He does. He knew Abraham's. And Rahab's. He knows all hearts, inside out and to their very depth. The point is, other *people* don't know; they have to see it demonstrated.

But—but!

No buts. Don't be the kind of person who must be explained ("She's really very nice when you get to know her"). Or the kind who has to explain himself ("I have an inferiority complex; that's why I'm so nasty"). Or the kind who lives in a vacuum ("He opens the door and nobody comes in").

James won't let you off the hook. He ends up tersely with a real stopper: "'Yes, faith without action is as dead as a body without a soul.'"

Spiritually, when you're dead, you're dead. You can't fake it. And that's that.

Think

This exercise will take two columns (and a lot of courage): Make a list of what you are "saying" in various significant areas of your life. Now a list of what you are actually "doing" in these same areas. Tack it up where you can check it out occasionally —(in a very private place; you won't want anyone to see it for awhile, until you've shaped up).

Memorize James 2:17.

6

Caution:
tongues working

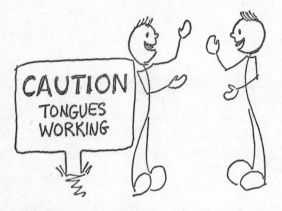

Shakespeare, who had something to say about almost everything, has an apt and pithy comment on the tongue: "He hath a heart as sound as a bell, and his tongue is a clapper; for what the heart thinks the tongue speaks."

An equally apt comment on somebody's wealthy mother-in-law who had a talent for saying the wrong thing: "She was born with a silver foot in her mouth."

But nothing has ever been written that can equal what James has to say about the tongue. He says it to the Christians in the church and he starts at the top:

"Don't aim at adding to the number of teachers, my brother, I beg you! Remember that we who are teachers will be judged by a much higher standard."

At first glance it would seem that James is talking to just the early church, for its members have been brought to heel before in many parts of the New Testament, for being incorrigible babblers. It seemed that everybody wanted to instruct. Ross suggests that "We wonder if he meant to suggest quietly that there were too many empty windbags among them already."*

But in a broader sense James is talking to anybody who *ever* preached a sermon or taught a class or wrote a book or led a meeting or "took over" a class to air his own views, or *in any way set himself up as a teacher*—and he's saying, *"Watch it!* We all make mistakes."

The word James uses means to "slip up." Some sage said, "Life is strewn with banana peels." Some sin is deliberate, but some of the things we've done that have brought us the most heartbreak have been the "slip-ups" when we were off our guard. "For we all make mistakes" means everybody who ever woke up in the morning. Touch him; if he's warm and breathing, he has "slipped up" some-

*The Epistles of James and John. Alexander Ross. Grand Rapids, Mich.: Eerdmans, 1954.

where along the line. "If we say we have no sin we deceive ourselves, and the truth is not in us" (I John 1:8, KJV).

AND IT WORKS BOTH WAYS

JAMES SAYS, DON'T

THE Establishment ADULTS TEACHERS etc.

Is this a "do it yourself" deal?

Is James giving us a "You Can Be a Success" lecture in verse 2: "But the man who can claim that he never says the wrong thing can consider himself perfect, for if he can control his tongue he can control every other part of his personality!"

No—James is saying: "If anywhere under the sun there *could* be found such a chap—" He has, if you'll pardon the reference, his tongue in his cheek. For there is no such person.

A little tongue——that important?

But the tongue is so small—how can it be so important? "That little piece of flesh between the jaws," wrote Luther.

And James answers: "Men control the movements of a large animal like the horse with a tiny bit placed in its mouth."

A bit is small, but you can steer a horse down the bridle path where he's supposed to go, or you can steer him into a tree and he'll hang you up on a limb.

"'Ships too, for all their size and the momentum they have with a strong wind behind them, are controlled by a very small rudder according to the course chosen by the helmsman.'"

A rudder is small, but you can steer the ship on its course where it's supposed to go, or you can steer it into the rocks and it *could* leave you clinging to the wreckage.

"'The human tongue is physically small, but what tremendous effects it can boast of!'"

The tongue is a many-splendored thing

Before we see what damage it can do, let us see a few of the guises it can take:

I might exaggerate a little. This is what is known as lying, if the fact or facts you added are distorting the picture so that your listener is deceived into thinking it was what it wasn't.

"I called the pastor and he wasn't in, and then I called her at 1:00 A.M. and she wasn't home yet. I understand they've been seen together before." (You called her at 11:00 P.M. and she wasn't in yet. And no, they were not out together.)

Unfortunately this is a true example.

Sometimes I'm hazy on some of the facts. This is what is known as lying, if the fact or facts you left out are distorting the picture so that your listener is deceived into thinking it was what it wasn't.

"She left the party with two boys and we didn't

see her the rest of the evening." (One of the boys was her brother, or didn't you notice?)

A ship's captain entered into his log every third or fourth day: "The first mate was sober today." He left out the fact that the first mate was sober every day. The first mate was fired.

Mary isn't home right now. Would you like to leave a rumour?

I use strong language. "Sometimes it takes strong language to get a point across. I prefer to call it 'salty.'"

This is what is known as profanity. Bob Timberlake (All-American football player—from University of Michigan) was working as a night watchman in a Chevrolet plant in Warren, Michigan. "I had a great deal of time to myself because half the night was spent walking between buildings and the other half sitting in an office building with nothing to do. Naturally there was plenty of time to think. One night I was thinking about a recent conversation with a fellow employee. I was appalled at my language. Every sentence had a 'cuss' word in it. So I thought, 'This is no way to talk, I'm going to change that right here; I'm never going to cuss again.' So after about three days of working on it, I never did cuss again."

This was before he became a Christian. In the weeks that followed, more and more things came to his mind about his personality which were wrong. He remembered sermons he had heard, and he began to think about God. And suddenly his goal— to be the most publicized quarterback in all times— became empty. He was searching for something more stable. He found it in the love of God. But even before he found it, God was already working on his tongue!

The chances are, if you are a Christian you do not use profanity as such—but are you addicted to the "minced oath"? According to Webster, "gosh" and "gee" are euphemisms for "God" or "Jesus." This is a subtle one for we do it without thinking of the significance of the word. And it's a hard one to argue about because even nice old ladies do it.

I let loose only when I'm with the guys. This is what is known as foul talk. Don't.

I say what I think, even if it hurts. Whether or not anybody asked for it? And even if it hurts someone else? "Well, one thing about me—I'm honest." (You are tactless and rude and hurting other peoples' feelings and putting them in their place gives you a feeling of importance.)

I don't embarrass anybody in front of other people. No, you talk about them *to* other people in their absence. This is what is known as backbiting or slander, depending on what you said.

Well I want them to get the point. This is known

as carping. You say it and say it and say it. They heard you the first time.

I try to improve people. This is what is known as criticism, and it had better be done in the right spirit. D.L. Moody's wife criticized him. She corrected his grammar and his spelling and his grooming and a dozen other things. But she did it with such charm and in such love that he never knew he was being criticized. At the end of his life he said he never ceased to be astonished that God gave him such a great ministry, and that God gave him his wife. They were in love till the day he died. She "improved" him with a gentle hand and a light touch. The personalities that have withered on the vine through criticism are legion.

Another version of this is "I like to see things done right."

I tell peoples' weaknesses to other people so we can pray about it. And don't you feel good about it?

This is what is known as the double-motive, or playing God, or slander, or breach-of-confidence, or malice, depending on what you tell, who you tell it to, and why you really told it.

I complain softly in a genteel manner. This is what is known as grumbling—to murmur or mumble in discontent. The advantage of this kind of complaining is that you can keep it up longer and do more damage. People don't jump on you as quickly as they would if you shouted. And there is nothing genteel about it.

I like to flatter people; it's nice. This is what is known as insincere praise, or death-by-sweet-talk. You are speaking with a forked tongue. If you don't mean it, look for your motives. Are you seeking to captivate the other person? Then you are giving him an unrealistic picture of himself. Are you hoping for flattery in return? If you become addicted to it, then you are getting an unrealistic picture of *yourself*. It's like the cartoon of the chap kneeling before his girl, proposing marriage. And she's saying, "Why Harry, I can hardly believe my well-formed shell-pink ears!"

I don't say anything wrong: I'm just a great old talker. This is what is known as being a bore, if you consistently "go past the ending."

"What makes it thunder?" a little girl asked her mother.

"I don't know too much about it," said the mother. "Wait till Daddy comes home. He'll be able to answer much better."

"Oh, no," said the little girl. "I don't want to know *that* much about it."

If somebody asks you what time it is don't tell him how to make a watch.

I stay out of trouble—I just don't talk. This is what is known as the cop-out. In tests to determine the damage today's loud music is doing to hearing sensitivity, it was discovered that eighty percent of the steady listeners suffer a temporary impairment and some might suffer permanent damage after a year of steady listening. Why do the young immerse themselves in noise? A Florida teen-ager explained: "The sounds embalm you. You don't know what to say to each other anyway. So why bother to talk?"

So you indulge in idle words and idle jesting, carefully schooling yourself not to say anything that

is going to make either you or anyone else *think*. If
you don't say anything you won't make any mistakes. It's like the young artist who presented for
sale the drawing of the little train chugging up the
hill. Only his caption, instead of being "I think I
can," was "Why should I?" It's the philosophy of
the times.

The treacherous world of "glances"

"But I didn't say a word! I just looked at him!"
The sins of the tongue don't always involve the
tongue. Sometimes a look is worth a thousand
words.

The Look of Annihilation. This is a frozen stare.
The brow is furrowed, the lips are firm with no
trace of a smile. Total destruction is in the air. It's
the look that engenders the comment, "If looks
could kill. . . ."

The Dead Pan. This look resembles fish on
chipped ice in a meat market. It is not infrequently
used on hapless teachers right after they've made a
point. It means you do not want to communicate
and are making no bones about it.

The Martyr's Mask. This is a look of extreme
pain. Biting the lower lip helps. Tears, if this fails.

The Deadly Squint. This look involves the jaw,
which is set firm. The eyes are narrow and menac-
ing. The mouth is a straight line. It means, "Do it,
or else," or, "Don't do it, or else."

The Resigned Look. The eyes are rolled back and
the mouth moves in wordless monologue. What it is
saying is anybody's guess.

Tinder is the tongue

James has told us that the tongue can do tre-mendous damage. Let's read on:

"'The human tongue is physically small, but what tremendous effects it can boast of! A whole forest can be set ablaze by a tiny spark of fire, 'and the tongue is as dangerous as any fire, with vast po-tentialities for evil. It can poison the whole body; it can make the whole of life a blazing hell.'"

The picture of a forest fire is a well-known one. We are brought up as children to prevent it if possi-ble and dread it if it occurs. A child on a camping trip was sent to the foot of the camp to empty some garbage in a container. As he was going through some brush, a small animal scampered by and made a noise. The child's father heard him whisper, "Is that you, Smokey?" Forest fires are so dreaded that we indoctrinate our children to prevent them as soon as they can understand. Outside the Word of God, there is little to impress us with the incalcula-ble damage the tongue can do.

Like a forest fire, the devastation is far-reaching. A careless word, a nasty rumor, a bit of slander— can ruin a person many miles away from the source. It is uncontrollable. Once the "spark" is dropped and the fire starts, the harm is done, and you can't get the "spark" back.

But this "tinderbox" does not do its damage only to other people. Your tongue can indeed "trip *you* up." For James says, "It (the tongue) can poison the whole body; it can make the whole of life a blazing hell." You cannot hurt others without hurting yourself.

It can't be done

Now James answers the question raised in verse 2. "But the man who can claim that he never says the wrong thing can consider himself perfect, for if he can control his tongue he can control every other part of his personality!" Read on:

"'Beasts, birds, reptiles and all kinds of sea creatures can be, and in fact are, tamed by man, ⁸but no one can tame the human tongue. It is an evil always liable to break out, and the poison it spreads is deadly.'"

We are a bundle of contradictions

It shows up in all our behavior. Paul laments the fact in the seventh chapter of Romans: "My own behavior baffles me. For I find myself not doing what I really want to do but doing what I really loathe . . . I don't accomplish the good I set out to do, and the evil I don't really want to do I find I am always doing."

Nowhere is this bundle of contradictions more evident than in the tongue:

"'We use the tongue to bless our Father, God, and we use the same tongue to curse our fellow men, who are all created in God's likeness. ¹⁰Blessing and curses come out of the same mouth—surely, my brothers, this is the sort of thing that never ought to happen!'"

It is told that there once lived a king in Egypt

who summoned his high priest and asked him to send him the best and the worst parts of the next sacrificed animal. The priest sent him the animal's tongue, together with a papyrus reading: "The tongue is the best part, for it carries the soothing words of friendship and the whisper of love; and it also is the worst part, for it bears the sting of hate and humiliation."

"Look at nature!" James goes on:

""Have you ever known a spring give sweet and bitter water simultaneously? "Have you ever seen a fig tree with a crop of olives, or seen figs growing on a vine? It is just as impossible for a spring to give fresh and salt water at the same time."

These same inconsistencies of the tongue plagued the saints of old. Peter cried, "Even if it means dying with you I will never disown you" (Matthew 26:35) and was denying Christ before the night was out with oaths and curses (Matthew 26:69-75).

And John—the same John who later wrote "Little children, love one another"—wanted to call down fire from heaven to burn up a Samaritan village (Luke 9:51-56).

It starts in the heart

Let's go back to Shakespeare for a moment. "He hath a heart as sound as a bell, and his tongue is a clapper; for what the *heart* thinks the tongue speaks."

But *can* the tongue be controlled?

Well, like diabetes, it can be controlled but not cured. Here is the Rx:

Look to your heart. "For a man's words depend on what fills his heart" (Matt. 12:34). "Keep thy heart with all diligence; for out of it are the issues of life" (Proverbs 4:23).

Talk to God about it. Ask Him earnestly to help you with it. "Set a watch, O Lord, before my mouth; keep the door of my lips" (Psalm 141:3). "Let the words of my mouth, and the meditation of my heart, be acceptable in thy sight, O Lord, my strength, and my redeemer" (Psalm 19:14).

Is it a losing battle?

Humanly speaking, it is. But with a Christ-controlled heart—no. It's a battle all right, and one you'll always have to fight. Let's look at it this way. You may lose a *skirmish* now and then, but if you are in earnest, the victory can be yours.

What's in it for me?

The trouble you will avoid will astound you. Your human relations in every area will improve. No more twinges like the ones you used to get when you knew you had cut somebody up into little pieces too short to hang up. You'll find that people you thought were impossible to get along with, are not so bad after all. And you will be honoring your Lord.

Think

1. Why do some people feel the need to use profanity?

2. Do you allow yourself little white lies? Justifiable lies?

3. Do you think a Christian should ever sue another person for slander?

4. If you were slandered, what course would you take?

7
It's a crime to be sharp?

You belong to one of the sharpest generations ever born since civilization began. The dictionary says that you are keen, eager, lively, brisk, spirited, alert, astute, attentive, clever, discriminating, discerning, perspicacious, observant, sensitive, quick to reason and understand.

Now a sharp mind is a gift from God, just as surely as a talent for music is, or a flair for art. And surely, if He has seen fit to give you such a gift, it behooves you to use it wisely. Gifts are one thing; how to use them, quite another.

"If all else fails, follow the instructions"

This is trade jargon. Manufacturers who make things that have to be put together are fond of saying it. They try to make their instructions explicit, but they know full well that the people who buy their products will try to put the thing together by themselves. It is in our human nature to plunge in and *do* it, whatever it is—for we are perfectly sure we know how—and then turn to the instructions sheepishly at last, following "Match AA to BB, making sure that—" Ugh.

It's humiliating business to have to admit that we took the wrong turn somewhere and messed the thing all up, and that the instructions were right after all.

But "instructions" are made for idiots!

"I could put the thing together in half the time it would take if I followed the instructions!" Perhaps you could. The manufacturer writes the instructions for people who don't know "AA" from "BB," or what to do next. (And sometimes they are so complicated or so vaguely written we wish heartily that the guy who wrote them was put in solitary for a month to try to figure them out.)

But we are talking about a gift from God and how He wants you to use it. With a gift like this, your potential is unbounded. Your opportunities are such to boggle the imagination. And your responsibilities are grave and awesome. You can do no better than to go to His Word and examine it and see for yourself what the instructions are, so you can use it to the best advantage.

Okay—I'm with it so far—what else?

If you're "with" the whole concept, are you willing to take it step by step? If you do, you'll see why being sharp is not enough; there's more to it. God says so, and He's very explicit about it. And if you learn some things you didn't already know, don't be embarrassed. Many so-called adults don't know them either. And some of them go to their graves without ever finding them out.

Step one: "take AA"—

"AA" is *knowledge*, and it would seem to be the answer to everything. We are indoctrinated with this little goodie from our childhood. From the time our mother takes us off to that strange realm of chalkdust and blackboards, and we face Miss Waste-

114

basket, grim or smiling, as the case may be, we learn that knowledge is a jewel of great price. It is an acquaintance with facts, truths, principles, and the way to make this acquaintance is to study, to observe, to investigate. But as necessary as it is, it isn't the answer to everything.

—And match it to "BB"—

We're back to being sharp. It means to latch onto the knowledge at our disposal; it would seem to be the golden key to success in life. All the knowledge in the world would do us no good if we were not sharp enough to absorb it. But one thing more is required.

Wisdom? What's that? And who needs it?

Wisdom is the ability to take the facts and relate them to your life, to *put them into action.* The word has been knocked about considerably and in our modern vocabulary it has come to mean a great many other things besides—get wise, get wise to, put someone wise, wise up—until we scarcely recognize it any more. But it still means what it always did; assimilate the facts and work them out in your conduct.

So you can have a quick intelligence and acquire knowledge, but if you cannot relate this knowledge to your life you can still be an emotional and spiritual infant.

We cannot think of wisdom without thinking of

Solomon. When God appeared to Solomon in the night and said, "Ask what I shall give thee," Solomon was confronted with a staggering decision. Just ask? Anything? Riches—wealth—honor—long life—*anything?* The possibilities were staggering! And Solomon's choice was a most unlikely one. He asked for wisdom and knowledge so that he would be able to rule over the great nation of Israel. That's all. Just wisdom and knowledge. God gave him what he asked for, and yes, riches—wealth—honor —and long life too. God gave him more than any mortal could dream of, much less use up in a lifetime. But of all the things Solomon got from God, he prized the most what he'd asked for in the first place. For he wrote much later and after much living: "Wisdom is better than rubies; and all the things that may be desired are not to be compared to it" (Proverbs 8:11).

Wisdom, then, is a gift from God, and He showers it generously upon us, worthy and unworthy alike. We all have the ability to take the facts at our disposal and relate them to our lives.

Then what's the problem?

There would seem to be none. From Miss Wastebasket on, we acquire knowledge, most of us are smart enough to do it passably well, and most of us have the wisdom to work what we've acquired into our conduct. What then is amiss? The problem is *the way we do it.* And this is exactly what James is talking about.

But James is talking to Christians

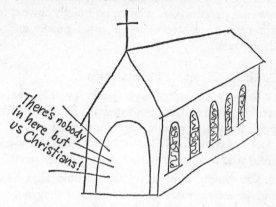

There's nobody in here but us Christians!

Yes, James is talking to the church. He's talking about wisdom. He's talking about *two kinds*. And there's the rub. He says:

James 3:13-18

¹³ᶜ"Are there some wise and understanding men among you? Then your lives will be an example of the humility that is born of true wisdom. ¹⁴But if your heart is full of rivalry and bitter jealousy, then do not boast of your wisdom—don't deny the truth that you must recognize in your inmost heart. ¹⁵You may acquire a certain superficial wisdom, but it does not come from God—it comes from this world, from your own lower nature, even the devil. ¹⁶For wherever you find jealousy and rivalry you also find disharmony and all other kinds of evil. ¹⁷The wisdom that comes from God is first utterly pure, then peace-loving, gentle, approachable, full of tolerant thoughts and kindly actions, with no

breath of favoritism or hint of hypocrisy. [18]And the wise are peacemakers who go on quietly sowing for a harvest of righteousness—in other people and in themselves."

Earthly wisdom: Rx for confusion

There is a wisdom, says James (v. 15), that is worldly, unspiritual, motivated by the devil: "You may acquire a certain superficial wisdom, but it does not come from God—it comes from this world, from your own lower nature, even from the devil."

The symptoms of this malady would fill a book, but James mentions only a few, and they are the ones most applicable to church life.

Jealousy The King James Version calls it envy. The two words have become interchangeable, but there is a subtle difference. Jealousy says, "I wish I had what you have. Whether or not you deserve to have it is not the consideration. I just resent that you have it and I don't." Then too, jealousy has a peculiar connotation of its own that has to do with our friendships, and it's worth mentioning. We have a friend; we lose a friend to someone else. Or we have a friend and we suspect that we are about to lose him to someone else. The latter is worse (if possible) than the former, for the agony of suspecting and not knowing, the uncertainty of whether we are going to win or lose can result in some of the darkest hours in our lives. The knowing is sometimes easier to bear in the end, if we can adjust to it. But more often than not, we don't adjust. Instead of giving it to God and accepting it as His will, we leave it inside to fester until hate sets in where love once was and the result is turmoil.

The kind of jealousy that we call envy is simply a feeling of ill will at seeing another's superiority or advantages or success. And it says, "I wish I had what you have and furthermore you have it by some fluke and don't deserve it and I hate your insides." Along with it goes the nasty thought of how nice it would be if you got toppled off your high and lofty place. It's not unlike the old game "King of the Hill" we played when we were kids—the object was to knock him *off*. We hope secretly that circumstances will do it, and if they don't seem disposed to, we are apt to hurry things along a bit and take a hand in it ourselves. How? It's all too easy. "I think it would be best if she got out of the choir; her voice is good of course, but so *loud*—the choir would be better if it were better balanced." (She's a terrific soprano and really carries the choir, but if she weren't there perhaps you'd get a solo now and then.) Or, "It's really better with him out of the group. He's so *aggressive*—nobody else had a chance." (You manipulated him out of the group because he was tremendously popular and *you* didn't have a chance.) Or, "She is awfully pretty but her taste in clothes!" (She is awfully pretty.) Or, "I didn't think to tell her about the sing. Oh, *wasn't* she here last Sunday?" (You knew she wasn't.)

These are the more obvious ways to do it. There are more subtle ways, and our ingenuity knows no bounds, for envy conjures up every trick we have in the bag. The pity of it is that when we try to destroy the other person we end up destroying ourselves.

Selfish ambition. This one is deadly because it has so many cover-ups. Assuming responsibility is one. This could mean riding roughshod over anybody who happens to be in the way to assume responsibility in an area where you weren't invited. Resourcefulness is another. This could mean finding devious methods of getting your way when you're blocked. Contributing is another. This could mean forcing your ideas on the chairman of the committee you are *not* on and sulking if you can't have your way. The list lengthens, interminably. Initiative and assuming responsibility and resourcefulness and contributing are noble attributes if they are done with the right motive. But if your motive is selfish ambition, you are wrong even when you're right. You can't win.

Rivalry. You don't like the way the sings are going? Set up your own sing with your own little group. You don't like the gang at the Saturday breakfasts? Set up your own little breakfast in your basement family room, and invite a select few. This is the stuff that "splits" are made of. "I am of Paul," . . . "I am of Apollos," . . . "I am of Peter"—these kinds of splits. You're all still in the church and you really haven't done anything *bad.*

Haven't you? James insists that you have stirred up a hornet's nest of trouble. [16]"For wherever you find jealousy and rivalry you also find disharmony and all other kinds of evil."

And the King James puts it: "Where envying and strife is, there is confusion and every evil work."

So no matter how you read it, it bodes no good, you have hindered the Spirit of God, you are being "wise" on your own steam. You can give your class or even your church a bad case of vapor lock* that could last for years.

Heavenly wisdom: Rx for peace

[17]"The wisdom that comes from God is first utterly pure, then peace-loving, gentle, approachable, full of tolerant thoughts and kindly actions, with no breath of favoritism or hint of hypocrisy."

It is pure. There go your ulterior motives. If you have the wisdom from God, you will have a new *sensitivity* that will help you recognize your motives for what they are, not what you thought they were. Jealousy and envy and ambition and rivalry will be rooted out for the culprits they are. This kind of wisdom bears the scrutiny of the Holy Spirit and comes out *pure.* No more stumbling about in the dark and wondering why you made such a mess of everything when you thought you were doing all right.

It is gentle. The dictionary says that to be gentle is to be kind and amiable. Not severe, rough, violent. Aristotle said about gentleness: "It is equity to pardon human failings, to look to the law-giver and not to the law, to the spirit and not to the letter, to the intention and not to the action, to the whole and not to the part, to the character of the person in the long run and not at the present moment, to remember the good and not the evil...." Nothing

*An obstruction in the fuel line.

121

mealymouthed or insipid implied here. This trait belongs to the *great*.

It is peace-loving. And this does not mean "peace at any price" that keeps you on the fence, agreeing with whomever you might be talking to at the moment. The Greek word has a very special meaning —*right relationships between man and man, and between man and God.** Wisdom from God, then, is the kind that produces *right relationships.* This one alone could solve half your problems.

It is approachable. Sam Shoemaker,** in talking about witnessing to others about our faith, lays down some rules. And the first one is—*be a gentleman.* And he means it strictly in the sense of having good manners. Be willing to listen to the other fellow. He mentions Ralston Young, Red Cap 42 at New York's Grand Central Station: "He's at ease with people, forever putting them at ease. He seems always to say the right thing because he is feeling the right thing—not merely the pat, polite thing, but the word that warms people and brings them out and sets the stage for talking about spiritual matters." *It allows discussion and is willing to yield* . . . *(LNT).* It does not drag in personalities when you are dealing with principles, or drag in excuses when you are dealing with problems. It is, in short, willing to sit down and talk about it, and "face up" if necessary.

It is full of tolerant thoughts and kindly actions. Full of tolerance? Just put yourself in the other fel-

*William Barclay
**Under New Management. Grand Rapids: Zondervan, 1966.

low's place. Stop and think, if you had his genes and chromosomes, his parents and grandparents and his background, right or wrong, you would see the thing exactly as he does. There are some cultures where it is all right to eat people. It isn't *right* but it is so. And if you were born there, that's the way *you* would look at it. So don't knock your opponent down just because he does not agree with you. He isn't a Christian and he's knocking down your every argument? Remember how you felt before you became a Christian? Be tolerant to him!

And kindly actions? *Again?* Yes, again. James says it and says it; it must be important.

It has no breath of favoritism or hint of hypocrisy. This does not mean that you jump on people with such enthusiasm that you send them staggering backward. It does not mean that you "say what you think" no matter who gets hurt. If someone says of you, "He comes on strong," stop and ask yourself just *how* you are coming on strong. You may be in for a shock. If you're going to be honest and straightforward, remember that gentleness and courtesy go along with it; it's a package deal.

And, without hypocrisy? Yes, sincere, free from pretense.

Round and round we go: and watch it!

All of which brings us back to the first two verses, where James has given us a trouncing:

[18]"Then your lives will be an example of the humility that is born of true wisdom."

King James says "meekness."

Meekness means you do not feel compelled to defend yourself. You are teachable. You are willing to give up having your own way. Meekness is a positive quality; *only the strong can afford it.*

[14]"But if your heart is full of rivalry and bitter jealousy, then do not boast of your wisdom—don't deny the truth that you must recognize in your inmost hearts."

You have been the mainstay of the "youth group" yea these many years? You don't commit any gross sins? You put tracts in all your correspondence? You can make snap decisions in committee meetings at the drop of a gavel? You're always first to suggest Christmas baskets or caroling? And you feel pretty smug about it? *Now* who's phony? Go back and read the chapter again; you've missed something.

You can't lose

In this last verse, James sums up everything that true wisdom means. If you've got it, here's what you are and here's what you'll do. [18]"And the wise are peacemakers who go on quietly sowing for a harvest of righteousness—in other people and in themselves."

You will have peace with God. You've been teachable; you've faced up to things, and come to grips with the culprits that lurk in earthly wisdom.

You will have peace with other people. Your human relationships will improve. Some problems might still be there, but the confusion is gone.

And you will have peace with the rascal who is giving you more trouble than anybody. Yourself.

The facts at-a-glance

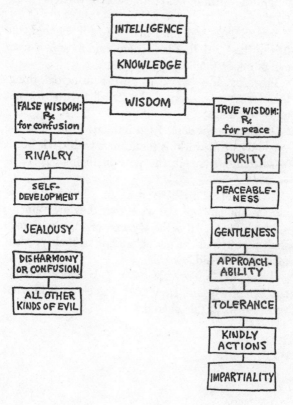

Think

1. *Heavenly wisdom.* Isaiah 11:2: "And the spirit of the Lord shall rest upon him, the spirit of wisdom and understanding, the spirit of counsel and might, the spirit of knowledge and of the fear of the Lord."

Job 28:28: "And unto man he said, Behold, the fear of the Lord, that is wisdom; and to depart from evil is understanding."

Proverbs 4:7: "Wisdom is the principal thing; therefore get wisdom: and with all thy getting get understanding."

2. *Earthly wisdom.* I Corinthians 3:19: "For the wisdom of this world is foolishness with God. For it is written, He taketh the wise in their own craftiness."

I Corinthians 3:20: "And again, The Lord knoweth the thoughts of the wise, that they are vain."

Isaiah 29:14: "For the wisdom of their wise men shall perish, and the understanding of their prudent men shall be hid."

3. Memorize Proverbs 14:8. Take stock of your concept of wisdom. How does it stack up with what you've read in this chapter?

8

War and peace

If we are to believe the news media, all youth is in active rebellion with a great gigantic uproar, substituting passion for knowledge, slogans for solutions and jargon for insight—against all adults who, if we are to believe the news media, jolly well deserve it. Unfortunately, the youth making the most noise—and the adults who deserve it—are the ones who get the press.

If the dust were to settle, we would find the vast

majority of young people attending their business, trying to get their educations, and preparing themselves to grapple with the problems they have inherited. And a vast majority of adults who are attending their business, grappling with the problems *they* have inherited and hanging onto the world until the next generation can grab hold of it.

The weary-go-round

The problems are inherited from the previous generation, who inherited them from the previous generation, all the way back to Adam and Eve. Some of them are solved, some of them are compounded. In either case, the youths of today, in a few years will find themselves askance, trying to answer the *next* crop of youths coming up. "You gypped us!" the new youths will cry. And the former youths will have passed the appalling age of 30 (the cutoff on credibility) and remember when *they* once cried "You gypped us!" to *their* elders, and round and round we go.

Maybe it will go away

A pop newspaper printed an edition in which all of the bad news was left out. All war news, all strife, all crime, all smears, all hate—every vestige of anything that might be disturbing, was gone. Nothing there but the goodies. And where the bad news might have been, there were only gaping empty spaces. And somehow those empty spaces looked strangely ominous, for the most insensate reader knew that not printing bad news did not make it go away.

There has always been strife—between nations and within nations—between individuals and, yes, *within* individuals. For the whole problem is due, ultimately, to the strife in the heart of man.

The Bible leaves no gaping blanks; it's all there. James gives us a bit of it in the first twelve verses of chapter four:

James 4:1-12

[1]"But what about the feuds and struggles that exist among you—where do you suppose they come from? Can't you see that they arise from conflicting passions within yourselves? [2]You crave for something and don't get it; you are murderously jealous of what others have got and which you can't possess yourselves; you struggle and fight with one another. You don't get what you want because you don't ask God for it. [3]And when you do ask he doesn't give it to you, for you ask in quite the wrong spirit—you want only to satisfy your own desires.

"'You are like unfaithful wives, flirting with the glamour of this world, and never realizing that to be the world's lover means becoming the enemy of God! Anyone who deliberately chooses to be the world's friend is thereby making himself God's enemy. ⁵Do you think what the scriptures have to say about this is a mere formality? Or do you imagine that this spirit of passionate jealousy is the Spirit he has caused to live in us? ⁶No, he gives us grace potent enough to meet this and every other evil spirit, if we are humble enough to receive it. That is why he says:

God resisteth the proud,

But giveth grace to the humble.

⁷"Be humble then before God. But resist the devil and you'll find he'll run away from you. Come close to God and he will come close to you. ⁸Realize that you have sinned, and get your hands clean again. Realize that you have been disloyal, and get your hearts made true once more. ⁹As you come close to God you should be deeply sorry, you should be grieved, you should even be in tears. Your laughter will have to become mourning, your high spirits will have to become heartfelt dejection. ¹⁰You will have to feel very small in the sight of God before he will set you on your feet once more.

¹¹"Never pull one another to pieces, my brothers. If you do you are judging your brother and setting yourself up in the place of God's Law; you have become in fact a critic of the Law. Yet if you start to criticize the Law instead of obeying it you are setting yourself up as judge, ¹²and there is only one

judge, the one who gave the Law, to whom belongs absolute power of life and death. How can you then be so silly as to imagine that you are your neighbor's judge?"

James does seem a bit gloomy here. And to make matters worse, he is again talking to the *church*.

"Hypocrites!" you bellow. "The church is full of hypocrites! I knew it all the time!"

Of course.

There are hypocrites in school too, but you're not going to drop out and miss your education. There are hypocrites in every strata of social life, but you're not going to become a hermit. There are hypocrites in business, but you're not going to bury your diploma when you get it, and join a breadline. To carry it to the ridiculous, you're not going to stay out of Macy's or Marshall-Field or Neiman-Marcus or Penney's or Woolworth's—or stop buying food in the markets, because some of the clerks are hypocrites. Like the Ancient Mariner's "water, water everywhere—" they're all over the place.

So let's get back to the case in point. James is talking to Christians. And he's making an earnest plea for us to examine ourselves in the light of God's Word.

¹"But what about the feuds and struggles that exist among you—where do you suppose they come from? Can't you see that they arise from conflicting passions within yourselves? ²You crave for something and don't get it; you are murderously jealous of what others have got and which you can't possess yourselves; you struggle and fight with one another."

Desire is the culprit

All things being equal, most of our desires seem legitimate and reasonable. We want money, popularity, possessions, recognition, gratification of bodily hungers, security, and a host of other seemingly harmless things to make us comfortable and happy. If we had no desires we would be like grubs, and who wants to be a glob of larva?

The point is not that we want these things, but that we want them too *much* or too *soon* or in the wrong way, or at the expense of someone or something else. And so we scheme and long and quarrel —and kill? Does James say kill? He that "*hateth* his brother is a murderer" (I John 3:15, KJV). Yes James says kill. We might be too Christian to even mutter in our hearts, "Oh, drop dead," but we do wish the hated rival would move to the uttermost parts of the earth and leave the field clear for us.

It is *overmastering* desire that James is talking about; the kind of desire that makes us slaves. And the crux of the whole messy business is that we desire the thing—whatever it is—more than we desire the will of God.

²"You don't get what you want because you don't ask God for it. ³And when you do ask he doesn't give it to you, for you ask in quite the wrong spirit —you want only to satisfy your own desires."

What do you want?

If what you want is based on comparisons and envy and greed, you will never be satisfied no matter what you get, or how much. There will always be someone else to envy, something else to possess, some other goal to achieve. This kind of want is like a bottomless pit; you can't fill it up.

What do you need?

Of course if what you want *is* based on comparisons and envy and greed, every little "want" will masquerade as a need. "Lord, I *need* this—I must have it now!" God is the only one who knows what you need. He made you unique, unlike any other person in the world. He loves you in a unique way; it is a very personal thing, this love. And the only "want" you can have that is absolutely 100% disaster-proof is to want His will for your life. If this is what you want, and you ask for it in faith, believing, He will give you what you need.

Rx for disaster

Oscar Wilde said, "Sometimes the only thing worse than not getting what you want, is getting it."

When the Israelites were in the wilderness, they were feeding on manna. It was what God wanted them to have; it was what they needed. But they wanted meat. Numbers 11 tells us how "the mixed multitude that was among them fell a lusting: and the children of Israel also wept again" (again? Yes, they were always weeping over something they wanted), "and said, Who shall give us flesh to eat?" Their diet of manna became loathsome to them. And their desire for meat became overwhelming. What happened? God finally gave them what they wanted. He sent them an abundance of meat, but they had no means of preventing spoilage and large numbers of them died of poisoning. When they finally pulled up camp and moved on, they named the place where they had been Kibroth-hattaavah— "graves of lust."

When they got to Kadesh-Barnea they had not learned their lesson. The Promised Land was in sight. It was what God wanted them to have. But they did not want to go over, for there were problems over there they did not want to face. "Would God that we had died in the land of Egypt!" they wailed, "or would God we had died in this wilderness" (Numbers 14:2)! What happened? They got what they wanted, and wandered in the wilderness for forty years with nothing *but* problems.

There was a boy who was studying for a career, when along came Alice. Now Alice was obviously not in God's will for this boy's life and he knew it. But he cried, "I must have Alice—I can't give up Alice!" So he *got* Alice and lived in frustration and regret for the rest of his life.

"We don't want manna—who shall give us flesh to eat?" "We don't want to go over into the Promised Land—there are too many problems!" "I must have Alice—I can't give up Alice!"

Sometimes the only thing worse than not getting what you want, is getting it.

The whole end of prayer should be "Thy kingdom come, *Thy will be done* —" and not "Thy kingdom stay away for awhile, *my desires be satisfied—*"

Friendship with the world—enmity with God

"'You are like unfaithful wives, flirting with the glamour of this world, and never realizing that to be the world's lover means becoming the enemy of God! Anyone who deliberately chooses to be the world's friend is thereby making himself God's enemy."

James is not saying that the world is a desert drear with absolutely nothing good about it. There is a story* about a Puritan who was out for a walk in the country with a friend. The friend noticed a lovely flower by the roadside. "Isn't that a lovely flower!" he said. And the Puritan frowned. "I have learned to call nothing lovely in this lost and sinful world," said he. And that took care of the flower.

*Barclay

With this sort of gloomy outlook, the question is, where do you stop?

Once there was a host who called his guest's attention to a lovely view of fields and stream and distant hills. "What pleasure," gloomed the guest, "does a heavenly man have in an earthly view?"

But later at dinner, this same guest asked for a second helping of some delicious peaches and cream. "And what pleasure," asked his host as he filled his dish, "does a heavenly man have in peaches and cream?"*

The world is God's creation; Jesus rejoiced in the beauty of it. It has been given to us to enjoy.

James is talking about the *forces* in the world which are completely indifferent to God or openly hostile to Him.

*Christian Joy, A. S. Loizeaux, Loizeaux Bros., N. Y

Here is where we have to define our terms. This is where Christians fight about what to fight about. There is this compulsion among Christians to set up a list of regulations, which always leads to confusion. For your list may not agree with the list of an equally fundamental and earnest church across town, or indeed with the person sitting next to you. And it certainly may not agree with the lists of your fellow Christians in other countries for their customs and cultures are different.

The dangers of the "list" are that you will invariably compare yours with others, which may lead to judging (strict and not-so-strict—the judging works both ways) and James tells us very plainly that we are not to play God (vs. 11,12). Or you may become so involved with the list and put so much importance upon it that your *list becomes your Christianity.*

It is well to remember that "selfishness in *any* form, whether it be the love of pleasure, self-gratification or arrogant self-seeking, is all 'friendship with the world'; and for the time being it causes the Christian to be at war with God."* So you can be just as guilty as the other fellow even though your list allows you to go nowhere but to church. More "arrogant self-seeking" is perpetrated in church than this world dreams of.

Dr. Jowett says: "Worldliness is a spirit, a temperament, an attitude of soul. It is life without high callings, life devoid of lofty ideals. It is a gaze horizontal, never vertical. Its motto is 'Forward,' never 'Upward.' Its goal is success, not holiness. Hearing no mystic voices, it is destitute of reverence. It never bows in rapt and silent wonder in the secret place. It experiences no awe-inspiring perceptions of a mysterious Presence. It has lusts, but no supplications. It has ambition, but no aspiration. God is not denied. He is forgotten and ignored."**

So when you're thinking fun-for-me, success-for-me, satisfaction-for-me, no-time-for-God—you are thinking "worldly." Color it black.

God, jealous?

The Living New Testament presents us with a different concept of verse 5: "The Holy Spirit, whom God has placed within us, watches over us with tender jealousy."

The word "jealousy" has come a long way from the original, and it has come a long way *down*. The kind of jealousy James is speaking of is the kind in

---

The General Epistle of James, Tasker. Eerdmans.
**Faith That Works,* John L. Bird. Zondervan. (Jowett, "Apostolic Optimism," p. 81.)

the Ten Commandments: "I the Lord thy God am a jealous God" (Exodus 20:5). "Thou shalt worship no other god: for the Lord, whose name is Jealous, is a jealous God" (Exodus 34:14). "The Greek word has in it the idea of hot and burning heat. God loves men with such a passion that He cannot bear any rival love within the hearts of men. He must receive from us a love which is beyond all earthly devotion."*

This is the most amazing and awesome truth in the whole book of James, indeed in the whole Bible. *God loves you, personally, that much!*

"The Holy Spirit . . . watches over us . . ."

Yes. And teaches us. And guides us. The Holy Spirit of God will tell you what your "do's and don'ts" should be. He will convict you of the most obvious don'ts (like feeding your mind with garbage) and the more subtle don'ts (like arrogant self-seeking) and the *most* subtle don'ts (like being proud of your own humility).

"But let's get back to this love God expects of me. I don't want to leave that point yet. Because I might as well admit right now that I'm not up to it. I start out all right in the morning, but I'm off my course by break. And while we're at it, I'm not so sure about those do's and don'ts, either."

Demand and supply

God knew you wouldn't be "up to it" before He ever made the demand. His demand for allegiance goes hand in hand with His supply of grace. "The

*Barclay

140

love of God is shed abroad in our hearts by the Holy Ghost which is given unto us" (Romans 5:5, KJV).

God never makes any demands that He will not give you the strength to meet.

"'No, he gives us grace potent enough to meet this and every other evil spirit, if we are humble enough to receive it. That is why he says:
God resisteth the proud,
But giveth grace to the humble.
"'Be humble then before God."

If you recognize that you need help, and ask for it, you'll get it. If you are too proud to know your own need or recognize your own shortcomings, you won't; it's as plain as that.

"How does it work?"

"All right. I know I need help. I ask for it. God gives me strength. Now what do I do with it? Or is it a passive sort of thing?"

No it isn't a passive sort of thing. And it isn't a cringing sort of thing either. It's an active sort of thing—a strength intended to give you dauntless courage. What do you do with it?

"Resist the devil and you'll find he'll run away from you."

In Bunyan's *Pilgrim's Progress*, Christian meets the devil at one point in the story, and the result is a classic picture of this verse in James.

"Where have you come from?" asked Satan, "and where do you think you're going?"

"I've come from the world," said Christian, "and I'm on my way to heaven."

"From the world, eh?" said Satan. "Then I perceive that you are one of my subjects. All that country is mine. I'm prince of it."

"I was indeed born in your dominions; but your service was hard and your wages such as a man could not live on; for the wages of sin is death."

"Ah," said Satan, "is that so? Well I'll tell you what I'll do. You go back, and I promise to give you —eh—whatever our country can afford."

"But I belong to the King!"

"Come, come," said Satan. "It's quite the common thing for those who have professed themselves His servants to give Him the slip after awhile and return again to me. Why don't you do it too, and all shall be well, I promise you."

Christian thought a moment. "But I *like* His service," he cried, "and I like His wages. And his servants. And His government, and yes, His *company* better than yours. So don't try to persuade me. I *want* to follow Him."

"Ah," said Satan sadly, "what a pity. You know of course that His servants have nothing but trouble. *Nothing* but trouble. And does He jump to deliver them? Ha!"

"He may not 'jump,' as you say, for a good reason. To try their faith. To make them strong. Sometimes He has reason to wait."

Satan ignored this. "*I* deliver those who faithfully serve me, by my power—"

"Power?"

"Power or fraud—what difference does it make? I deliver. And so I will deliver you."

"They shall have their deliverance in our Prince's good time," said Christian stubbornly.

Satan tried another tack. "You've already been unfaithful to Him," he said. "How do you expect to receive wages of Him?"

"Where have I been unfaithful?"

And Satan proceeded to name where and when, in every humiliating detail.

"Everything you say is true," said Christian, "and there's more that you left out. But my Prince is merciful and ready to forgive."

Then Satan broke out in a rage. "I hate this Prince!" he roared, "I hate His person—I hate His laws—I hate His people! I've come out on purpose to withstand you!"

"Beware what you do," said Christian, "for I'm in the King's highway: watch it!"

Whereupon Satan straddled the highway in front of Christian and the fight began. There isn't space to tell it all here, but the evil one's darts flew as thick as hail and Christian was exhausted and wounded and finally fell. Now the interesting thing about this fight was that when Christian dropped his sword* Satan nearly did him in. But when Christian picked it up again, he was able to leap to his feet and cry, "Rejoice not against me, O mine enemy: when I fall I shall arise!"** With that, he gave Satan a deadly thrust with the sword and the culprit fled.

*The sword is the Word of God.
**Micah 7:8

143

"Come close to God and he will come close to you." And this does not mean a step or two—it means all the way. When the prodigal son decided to go back to his father, he went *all the way*. But when he was yet a long way off, his father saw him coming—*and ran to meet him*.

Is this any way to walk?

²⁰"Realize that you have sinned, and get your hands clean again. Realize that you have been disloyal, and get your hearts made true once more. ⁹As you come close to God you should be deeply sorry, you should be grieved, you should even be in tears. Your laughter will have to become mourning, your high spirits will have to become heartfelt dejection. ¹⁰You will have to feel very small in the sight of God before he will set you on your feet once more."

"This is just the sort of thing that keeps people away from the church. Long-faced Christians, looking as if they'd been baptized in vinegar—"

James is not talking about your *walk*; he's talking about your *repentance*. He's merely telling you to straighten up, *inside and out*—and *mean* it!

The prodigal son said, "Father, I have sinned against heaven and you, and am not worthy to be called your son—" But his father said to the servants, "Quick! Bring the finest robe in the house and put it on him. And a jeweled ring for his finger; and shoes! And kill the calf we have in the fattening pen. We must celebrate with a feast!" And they began to get the festivities going.

The Bible is filled with admonitions to be glad, to be merry, to laugh. "A merry heart doeth good like a medicine" (Proverbs 17:22). "And all the people went their way to eat, and to drink, and to send portions, and to make great mirth, because they understood the words (of God) that were declared to them" (Nehemiah 8:12). "Till he fill thy mouth with laughing, and thy lips with rejoicing" (Job 8:21).

The prodigal son was merry *after* he got home; there is no doubt that he shed many tears on the way.

What's in it for me?

This whole chapter boils down to one word: choice. There's a war going on in your personality—your desires or His—your will or His. The skirmishes will go on for as long as you live. He gives you the strength to win—a skirmish at a time.

The only "want" you can have that is absolutely 100% disaster-proof is to want His will for your life. And what will you get? Peace with God—and a better life than you could have possibly chosen for yourself.

Think

Memorize verses 6 and 7.

Make a list of your needs. Examine each one carefully and lop off the "wants" on your list that are masquerading as needs.

Let's assume your goals are perfectly legitimate and within the framework of God's will for you;

how are you working toward them? What methods are you using to obtain them?

Take a look at Psalm 36:4,5. (Might be a good idea to memorize these verses; they're life changers.) Can you define "desires" in the context of these verses?

Think through the consequences of a strong desire in your life. If you got what you wanted, what might the ramifications be? Would getting it (as Oscar Wilde said) be worse than not getting it?

What is your list of "do's and don'ts"? Is it a carbon copy of the mores of your peer group? Or are you doing some of your own thinking in the light of God's Word?

9

There was this plan . . .

There were these men. . .

. . . walking, perhaps, along the narrow streets of the busy city, through the teeming crowds, past the shops that line the streets, past the wares out on the pavement—nuts, grapes, sheep, spices, pigs' feet, milk in goatskin bags, guts—

"We'll go to Scythopolis—". . . dates, grape leaves, silks, olives, camels' feet—

"—tomorrow, and set up a business—" . . . rugs, bread, wine, oils, water jugs, camels' heads—

"—and stay there a year, and make a profit—"

Or there were these men, sitting, perhaps, in a

busy seaport in the midst of ships—big ships, middle-sized ships, old and dirty ones, bright new ones with names of heathen gods in glittering letters on their bows.

"We'll go to Rome—"

Some ships with white sails—some with dirty sails of no color at all—some with brilliant sails of orange and yellow and scarlet—

"—and stay there a year—"

And noises. Shouting, grumbling, laughing, the whack of the shipwright's mallet, the creak of pulleys hauling cargo aboard, the squawking of parrots—

"—and make a profit—"

These were the kinds of men James used for his illustration, and he paints a graphic picture:

James 4:13-17

[13]"Just a moment, now, you who say: 'We are going to such-and-such a city today or tomorrow. We shall stay there a year doing business and make a profit'! [14]How do you know what will happen even tomorrow? What, after all, is your life? It is like a puff of smoke visible for a little while and then dissolving into thin air. [15]Your remarks should be prefaced with, 'If it is the Lord's will, we shall still be alive and shall do so-and-so.' [16]As it is, you get a certain pride in yourself in planning your future with such confidence. That sort of pride is all wrong.

[17]"No doubt you agree with the above in theory. Well, remember that if a man knows what is right and fails to do it, his failure is a real sin."

"Look here," says James. "Come now, wait a minute—let's stop and consider this matter." Are you living your life as if God had absolutely nothing to do with it? What presumptuousness! What brazen effrontery! What nonsense! James is perhaps thinking of a parable our Lord told one afternoon on a hillside when "the crowds had gathered in thousands, so that they were actually treading on one another's toes" (Luke 12:1).

"Once upon a time a rich man's farmland produced heavy crops," said Jesus. "So he said to himself, 'What shall I do, for I have no room to store this harvest of mine?' Then he said: 'I know what I'll do. I'll pull down my barns and build bigger ones where I can store all my grain and my goods and I can say to my soul, Soul, you have plenty of good things stored up there for years to come. Relax! Eat, drink and have a good time!' But God said to him, 'You fool, this very night you will be asked for *your soul*'" (Luke 12:16-20)!

In making his plans for his future, the "fool" in our Lord's story forgot that the length of his life was something he had nothing to say about. And he found out to his dismay that he was not going to be around to enjoy what he was planning.

There was this king . . .

His name was Hezekiah, and he "walked uprightly before the Lord." He had hastily rebuilt the walls of Jerusalem when the Assyrians had besieged it—he had dug a great conduit to bring water in from a spring outside—his workers had brought that water 1750 feet through solid rock, into the pool of Siloam

150

inside the city walls—

But one day Hezekiah fell ill, and the prophet Isaiah came to him and told him the Lord had said he was going to die.

Now Hezekiah had a remarkable record of fantastic feats, all done in the will of God. "I have walked before thee in truth and with a perfect heart" (II Kings 20:3), he reminded God. "There is much yet to do. Give me more time!" And God did. God promised Hezekiah fifteen more years.

Now this is a very amazing thing. Here is a man who knew exactly how much more time he had to live. As far as we know, he was the only man on record who did.

What he did with those fifteen years is an interesting story (II Kings 20:8-19) and there isn't space to tell it here, but his heart became "lifted up" (puffed up, as it were) and he made more mistakes in those few years than he had made in all his other years put together.

You may have a few hours, like the fool in the parable. You may have fifteen years like Hezekiah. You may have fifty. Or even sixty. James is saying that you do not *know*—and this is the point.

There was this racer. . .

He raced boats. He planned to crack 300 miles an hour, and then he planned to quit racing. He did crack 300 miles an hour, and he did quit racing— but not the way he had planned. At 310 miles an hour Donald Campbell's jet hydroplane, Bluebird, disintegrated. There was a picture of the disaster in our national magazines—Donald Campbell and all his plans gone up in a puff of smoke.

There was this young girl. . .

A girl named Jayne wrote to the "Teen-to-Teen" section of *Campus Life*. While Jayne was in the hospital for surgery, a girl her own age was in the habit of coming over from across the hall, and they'd talk together. On the morning Jayne was discharged she had to go downstairs for a partial cast. On her way back to her room, she stopped across the hall to say goodbye. "As I wobbled back to my room, I stopped across the hall to show Mary my newest. But the bed was empty, and they told me she had left that morning.

"Only when I got home did my mother tell me that Mary had passed away! I had talked to her about Christ, although she seemed indifferent at the time and said she had 'heard all that religion.' But a few days after the funeral, her mother came to see me. 'I want you to know,' she said, 'what Mary told me before she went into a coma. She told me you and she had talked about Christ, and everything was okay.'"

"How do you know," says James, "what is going to happen tomorrow? For the length of your lives is as uncertain as the morning fog—now you see it; soon it is gone" *(LNT)*.

What then? Can't I make plans?

"Do I go about in a pall of gloom, always thinking, 'If the Lord wants me to, I shall live?'" No, you go about in joy and confidence, making plans—immediate plans and long-range plans—thinking, "If the Lord wants me to I shall live or *do so-and-so*" (see v. 15). You don't have to be like the chap in the cartoon who says "I never bring a lunch to work —in case I get fired before noon."

This or that

And again it's a matter of choice.

Making your own plans . . . "Lord, I thought maybe I'd forget about college for awhile—not skip it—just postpone it for a year, maybe two—and just kick around—get a job and have some fun and freedom and then get back to the grind a little later when it's more convenient—"

"I thought I might like to be a missionary—try it for a few years—far-off places have always intrigued me—"

"I thought I might keep going steady with Jack for awhile, maybe even get married—"

"I want a career more than anything else—I don't know exactly *what*—but it would be fun to have a career and my own money and freedom—"

"I just want to bum around—well not *bum* around, but sort of float around—there isn't any hurry—what if I do make a few mistakes? I can always go back and start again—and maybe I'll learn something—experience is the best teacher—maybe I'll even be the wiser for it—"

"I thought I might try my luck at this—I've always had a flair for it—"

The problem with this kind of thinking is that you cannot go back and do it over again. You may have "instant replay" but you can't go back. Anyone who has ever watched sports on TV knows what instant replay is. You see spectacular plays or crucial plays over again, to your delight or consternation, as the case may be. And you see controversial plays the way they really happened. There is hardly a football fan who cannot remember some pass reception in some big game where an official called it a touchdown but the camera, particularly in slow motion on the instant replay, showed clearly that the ball was caught outside the end zone. The fans booed it as they saw it. Or cheered it as they saw it. And the official called it as he saw it. But the instant replay had the last word.

You may look back and see the things sifted through the filters of your own desires and prejudices and protective instincts, or you may be realistic enough to really have "instant replay" and see the thing as it was—but in either case *you cannot go back and live it over again.*

And the sad truth is that now your choices are more limited. Now you must choose from what you have left. The ball was caught outside the end zone. You goofed. Where do you go from here? Well, God is merciful, God loves you, He will always love you —but look what *you* did. And what *you* did determines the rest of your life. The scope has narrowed down. Every choice you make now is contingent upon the choices you *made.* Now you pick up the pieces, He loves you, but you have limited Him. He can only work with what's left. You get another chance? Yes. But you don't get it the way it was; you get it the way it *is.*

Or choosing God's will for your life. David cried,

"Show me thy ways, O Lord, teach me thy paths. Lead me in thy truth" (Psalm 25:4,5).

And no half measures. It cannot be, "Your will, Lord—except for this one thing." Nor can it be, like Augustine's halfhearted prayer, "Lord, make me clean—but not now."

No, it's *all the way*. And could you put yourself in better hands? "He is . . . the upholding principle of the whole scheme of creation" (Col. 1:17).

And that includes *you*.

There were these people. . .

Don Moomaw of All-American football fame, planned to go with the Rams. But he planned "if the Lord wants me to." It turned out that the Lord wanted him to go into the ministry instead, and he obeyed. It is where he is now.

On the other hand, Cazzie Russell of All-American basketball fame planned to stay in basketball "if the Lord wants me to" and that is exactly where the Lord did want him to stay. And Cazzie's ministry is witnessing. He is known for his bull sessions in the Knickerbocker locker room, witnessing to the other members on his team. He is also known for his "disciplined practice and his tremendous enthusiasm." Which doesn't sound like sitting in a pall of gloom.

About his life and his success Cazzie says, "The money, the fame, the popularity . . . all these are transient and will pass with time. But faith is permanent. To live with God in *this* life is to live with Him in the next, and they haven't minted enough money to water down my faith the slightest degree."*

And then there is Bob Timberlake. And Felipe Alou . . .

These people, and untold thousands like them are going ahead with gusto and enthusiasm, taking a day at a time, knowing that their "times are in God's hands," and making their plans with the proviso—"if it is the Lord's will."

One more thing

"Oh, yes," says James. "And one more thing. Now you've been told. Now you know (verse 17). *Now* if you continue to live your life as if God had absolutely nothing to do with it—it is sin."

There was this plan. . .

God's plan—for you. What happened to it? What's happening to it? What's going to happen to it? It is up to you.

What's in it for me?

When you make your plans contingent upon God's will for your life, you automatically stop sweating over the obstacles in your path. A "closed door" is no longer the crushing blow it used to be. Life can actually take on a sense of adventure— what is the Lord up to now? He will never show you the complete pattern of your life, all wrapped up and very pat. If you have really chosen His will for you, He will give you sufficient light for the next

*Me, Cazzie Russell. New Jersey: Revell

step. And there is nothing gloomy about the fact that you do not have the promise of your next moment. And nothing new, either; you knew it all the time.

Think

1. Write down your long-range plan, *your* goal for your life. Make a list of your immediate plans. Do they check?

2. Write down what you believe God's plan is for your life. Make a list of your immediate plans. Do they check? Are there areas in your life that might militate against God's plan for your life? Do they seem harmless? Are they harmless in the light of what you've read in this chapter, James 4:13-17?

3. Are you praying in God's will? Check yourself against Ephesians 6:18; I John 5:14,15.

4. Go over your lists again. Which list do you have for your life? What checks? And which do you choose?

10

It's a sin to be rich?

As Christians we're apt to feel either of two ways about money. (1) We handle the subject rather gingerly, for we have a feeling of guilt about it—it seems to be somehow too horizontal and not quite right. Nice, but not *right*. (If we don't have it we somehow feel more spiritual, and if we do have it we get on the defensive.) Or (2) We equate it with God's blessing—if we do have it, like in the song, we "must have done something good" and if we don't have it we must have somehow slipped up somewhere.

Actually there's no reason for confusion about it, for nowhere in the Bible are riches condemned. And nowhere in the Bible are we told not to like money. We are simply told *not to like it too much*. God is very emphatic about this.

In the following verses, James is not denouncing all rich men indiscriminately. He's talking to the *ungodly* rich and he's denouncing them like an Old Testament prophet. Barclay says "Not even the most cursory reader of the Bible can fail to be impressed with the social passion which blazes through its pages. . . . There is no book which condemns dishonest and selfish wealth with such searing passion as the Bible does."*

Searing passion, indeed. This is a capital-labor speech and it's modern enough to be in one of today's newspapers. James does not start out this diatribe with his usual tender, "dear brothers." He says, "And now, you plutocrats . . ."

James 5:1-6

¹ᵃAnd now, you plutocrats, is the time for you to weep and moan because of the miseries in store for you! ²Your richest goods are ruined; your hoard of clothes is moth-eaten; ³your gold and silver are tarnished. Yes, their very tarnish will be the evidence of your wicked hoarding and you will shrink from them as if they were red-hot. You have made a fine pile in these last days, haven't you? ⁴But look, here is the pay of the reaper you hired and whom you cheated, and it is shouting out against you! And the cries of the other laborers you swindled are heard

*Barclay

by the Lord of Hosts himself. "Yes, you have had a magnificent time on this earth, and have indulged yourselves to the full. You have picked out just what you wanted like soldiers looting after battle. "You have condemned and ruined innocent men in your career, and they have been powerless to stop you."

This is strong language. In verses 2 and 3 James puts it in the present tense—"Your richest goods *are* ruined," etc. It's as good as done! And in verse 3, in the King James Version, he says their gold and silver will *rust*. Now anyone knows that gold and silver won't rust, but it's a neat way of saying how utterly worthless it will be. Even the most apparently indestructible things will lose their value. James is speaking of the ultimate valuelessness of all earthly things.

But what did it have to do with Christians?

"But James is writing this letter to Christians. The 'ungodly rich' would probably never get to read it or hear it." Probably not. It's a roundabout way of telling the poor Christians not to envy the rich, ungodly or otherwise. And warning the rich Christians lest they fall into the snare of letting their wealth become too important to them. Which takes care of everybody very tidily.

How does it apply to me?

The principle applies to you. And the principle is materialism. The dictionary tells us that materialism is "attention to or emphasis on material objects, needs, and considerations, with a disinterest in or rejection of spiritual values." It's that new cashmere, that car, that wardrobe, those records, that stereo—when they become more important to you than what God is trying to work out in your life if you'll drop your wallet long enough to listen. To concentrate on material things is to concentrate on what will ultimately be a delusion.

Money—slave or master?

Hetty Green was once the richest woman in America. At her death she was worth up to $100,000,000. But she padded herself with newspapers to keep warm in winter, she resold her morning newspaper after she'd read it, she sat up all night in the day coach rather than indulge in the luxury of a Pullman berth, she sorted out white rags from the colored ones in the attic of one of her warehouses because the junk man paid a cent a pound more for white rags. Most of her investments were in New York, but instead of buying a home there she lived in cheap lodging houses under assumed names so she would not have to pay income tax. And when she was on her deathbed at eighty-one her nurses were not permitted to wear uniforms, for old Hetty would never have died in peace if she'd suspected that she was paying expensive registered nurses' wages. Money was her master. She lived for it, worshiped it. It was more important to her than even the comforts it could buy.

The Wendel family was one of New York's richest—their holdings were valued at a hundred million dollars. A bachelor brother—John Gottlieb Wendel, and seven sisters.

John Gottlieb insisted on gas for lighting instead of electricity. No radios, no automobiles, no modern (at that time, modern) conveniences of any kind. Suitors for his sisters? Never! They were after the money. He told them not to call again. Only one sister married—and then, not until she was sixty. Georgianna, the most spirited of the sisters, fought against the restrictions and paid for it with a persecution mania and had to be sent away. Josephine lived alone in one of the country houses, surrounded only by servants. She dreamed that the house was filled with noisy happy children, and talked and played with them in her imagination. She even imagined her guests—and had dinner served and then changed places at the dinner table, pretending she was each guest in turn.

One by one they died—John and the sisters—until only Ella was left. The rooms of the dead were locked and the shutters closed, and Ella lived on in only the dining room and her bedroom and the huge bare room upstairs where she and her sisters had passed their lonely school days.

She lived on for years there, with only servants—and Tobey. Tobey was a French poodle, and he really *did* live it up. He slept in Ella's bedroom in a four-poster bed exactly like Ella's. And he ate his sumptuous meals in the dining room at a special table spread with a velvet cloth. And he had the only yard in the world worth a million dollars maintained especially for him to play in.

Then Tobey died. And Ella died. And what happened to all the money? Well, John Gottlieb Wendel had not made a will. He did not want "any lawyer making money out of his riches." Before the estate was finally settled two hundred and fifty lawyers were in on it, collecting fees to untangle the millions and set everything straight. The Wendel family had a hundred million dollars and it had not brought them one moment of happiness.

The only one who profited was a dog.

There was a woman once, who turned down a thousand proposals of marriage—many of them from very rich men. Even a prince. Yes, a prince followed her for years and begged her to marry him. And, incredible as it seems, even after she had reached her threescore years and ten, she was still getting proposals by mail—so many that her secretary did not even bother to show them to her.

Talk about the credibility cutoff at thirty! She rode a wild horse at forty—bought him cheap because his owner was afraid of him—did fancy diving when she was sixty-three—swam across Lake George in four hours then, too. Slept with a pad and pencil beside her bed so she could make quick notes for sermons if she woke up—

When she was old enough to be a grandmother, her dark red hair was streaked with grey—but she was sparkling, she was blazing—with enthusiasm and vivacity.

Who was she? Just Evangeline Booth, daughter of the founder of the greatest army that ever attacked an enemy—the Salvation Army—an army with thousands of officers, feeding the hungry at home and in far-flung countries—and spreading the gospel in eighty languages . . .

Money? Of course she had it. And she *used* it. But it was her slave. It was never her master.

Ed Studd was a wealthy sportsman in England who came to Christ in a most amazing and amusing way. "I bought a new horse," he told a wealthy friend one day. "And I'm going to race him. You'd better put some money on him. He's a winner."

A few weeks later Ed met his friend and asked him if he'd put any money on the horse (the horse indeed had won) and the friend said he had not. "You're a bigger fool than I thought," said Ed, "but to show you I'm a sport I shall take you to dinner and afterward we'll go anywhere you like."

What Mr. Studd did not know was that something very earthshaking had happened to his friend since they'd last met. His friend had gone to Ireland on business, had missed the last train home, had seen a sign on a marquee—*Moody and Sanky,* had thought it was an American vaudeville act, and had gone in to kill some time. And there he had been introduced to our Lord by the great evangelist D.L. Moody, and had come out of that theater never to be the same.

Mr. Studd and his friend went to dinner and afterward—

"Well, where would you like to go?" said Studd. "Anywhere you say."

"Very well, then. To the Queen's Theater."

"The Queen's Theater? Why those American evangelists are there! You can't be serious."

But his friend was serious. When they got there it was so crowded they couldn't get in. Mr. Studd was ready to leap back into their carriage with relief, but his friend scribbled a note to an usher saying that if they did not get in, he would never be able to get his friend back to such a meeting again. So they got seats. Folding chairs. On the platform. Right under D.L. Moody's nose!

That night Ed Studd was spun around and his sense of values was turned upside down and money never meant the same thing to him again. He met his Lord.

He let the Lord use his wealth and he let the Lord use himself. He lived only a few years after that night, but in those few years God was able to do more through him than He can through many Christians in a whole lifetime.

"But some of these things don't apply to me!"

"But wait a minute. If all this applies somehow to

me, I'm still hung up on two snags. One is verse four. 'Here is the pay of the reaper you hired and whom you cheated, and it is shouting out against you!' I know James is talking about employer-employee relationships and it works both ways. I get the concept all right, but I have this summer job and I've never cheated anybody."

Probably not. But you might give yourself a little checkup. Do you get to work on time? Are you habitually late? Only ten minutes or so? If you're a girl, do you save your hair-comb and your face until after you've checked in, and then go to the lounge to complete your grooming? For that matter, with hair the way it is, if you're a boy? What about your coffee break? The TV commercial that said "s-t-r-e-t-c-h your coffee break" was talking about gum, not minutes. And how many minutes (or hours?) do you spend hanging in office doorways or in corners, chatting? Are you ready to leave fifteen minutes early? Figure up all those minutes for the duration of your summer job. How much do you make an hour? How many dollars have you rooked from your employer?

"Okay, okay. But how about verse six? 'You have condemned and ruined innocent men in your career, and they have been powerless to stop you.'"

Go back and read Chapter 6—Caution: Tongues Working. Did you ever get a rival out of the way with a few well-chosen words? And did you ever say (or think) "I sure blew him out of the tub. Boy, I murdered him!" "Whosoever hateth his brother is a murderer" (I John 3:15). You could be right.

Money money everywhere

Yes, and the words that have been said about it would fill the air waves clear to the moon. And the words that have been written about it would fill the libraries of the world. What about it?

The con: "Away with it. That's the trouble with the establishment. Pick flowers. Love. And in time—"

This is what a very articulate (and very intelligent) chap cried out in a panel discussion on TV. "In time—" he cried, "the news media will know what we're talking about and will agree with us—"

What news media? TV? Radio? The newspapers? And who's going to pay for them? How? And with *what?* The argument goes down the drain so fast you can't catch it by the hair.

The pro: All things being equal, money has been around for a long time. And it seems to be here to stay. We can use it or abuse it. What is our duty as Christians?

Well, it boils down to a few points. And they could be worded in many ways, but basically they are these:

Get it honestly. This covers everything from filching, mooching, cheating, and outright stealing. Any way you look at it—whether you are stealing it outright or stealing it in more subtle ways—you are stealing it. Get it honestly.

Use it wisely. Even a cursory reading of any of our great Christian athletes will tell you that they did not get their success dropped from the sky. They worked for it. Many of them were of moderate means, or even poor. They got summer jobs, part-time jobs, *anything* to help them reach their goal. And some of them went hungry. They used what little money they had wisely. They budgeted (horrible word—means discipline) their money and it wasn't easy.

The moment of truth

When old Mount Vesuvius erupted in A.D. 79, there wasn't a person in Pompeii who thought about money. For Mount Vesuvius was erupting on Pompeii. The layers of ash and pumice that covered the city preserved everything in it to this present day. Great displays of wealth were found—silver and gold and pottery and jewelry and mosaics and the great Theater and the Temple of Isis. And the people were found there, too. And their food. And their pets. And their babies. Some of them were engaged in acts of living as if they'd had absolutely no warning of disaster. Others were in the act of fleeing—too late. From the skeletons of the priests in the Temple of Isis to the man on the street, there is mute evidence that in one blinding moment everything ground to a halt and the richest man in Pompeii couldn't buy his way out.

A place for everything—even money

There is nothing wrong with having money—and *liking* it. And there is nothing wrong with having and enjoying things. It's when material things get between you and God that your whole sense of values goes haywire, and God cannot get through to you. If you are sulking over what you cannot have, you are limiting what God wants to give you. If you are "setting your heart" only on the material things you do have, you are passing up the kind of riches that count for eternity. God wants you to like and appreciate money. But He does not want money to be your God.

Think

1. Make a list of the ways you might be filching people *other than* filching them out of money.

2. Do you repudiate the establishment, and feel that you are not materialistic? (Remember the definition of materialism: "Attention to or emphasis on material objects, needs and considerations . . .")

3. Take a look at the rest of the definition (". . . with a disinterest in or rejection of spiritual values"). How do you feel about it now?

4. Read I Timothy 6:7; Proverbs 13:7; 10:22.

11

Take the humbug out of your Christianity

One thing can be said for James—he certainly can write a letter to make you squirm. Just as you think you have everything squared away, he comes up with one more point. If you did not know that God is speaking to you in love, and for your own good, it would be easy to say of James: "He sure knows how to hurt a guy."

James 5:7-12

⁷"But be patient, my brothers, as you wait for the Lord to come. Look at the farmer quietly awaiting his precious harvest. See how he has to possess his soul in patience till the land has had the early and late rains. ⁸So must you be patient, resting your hearts on the ultimate certainty. The Lord's coming is very near.

⁹"Don't make complaints against one another in the meantime, my brothers—you may be the one at fault yourself. The judge himself is already at the door.

¹⁰"For our example of the patient endurance of suffering we can take the prophets who have spoken in the Lord's name. ¹¹Remember that it is usually those who have patiently endured to whom we accord the word 'blessed.' You have heard of Job's patient endurance and how God dealt with him in the end, and therefore you have seen that the Lord is merciful and full of understanding pity for us men.

¹²"It is of the highest importance, my brothers, that your speech should be free from oaths (wheth-

er they are 'by' Heaven or earth or anything else).
Your yes should be a plain yes, and your no a plain
no, and then you cannot go wrong in the matter."

In these verses, James makes three points. They
may seem unrelated but they are not. They all boil
down to one thing: You and your humbug.

"I won't take this lying down!"

"Be patient when people abuse you," James is
saying (verses 7-9)—and the kind of patience he is
talking about is self-restraint. He means "no retaliation." Life is not an Indian handwrestle and you
don't spend it trying to force the other fellow's arm
back down. The Authorized Version says "Grudge
not one against another."

James has said this before, but now he says it
with a sense of urgency. The Lord is coming! It's as
if James were saying, "What? Are you *still* at each
other's throats? *When the Lord is at the door?*"

The big grudge sludge

Grudge is a nasty word. Even phonetically, it is
dissonant, harsh, out of harmony. You put it in any
sentence and no matter how nice the sentence started out, it comes to a grinding halt, and stops, shiv-
ering. You've groused it up. It's a *mean* word; you
can't make anything pretty out of it. We speak of
"carrying a grudge" but we don't "carry" it actually
—we sort of wallow in a grudge sludge, picking our
feet up with ugly sucking sounds, and putting them
down again in the ooze. Yeaaaaauk!

The big grudge sludge

The old grudge beads

In the Middle East they have what they call "worry beads." Any Arab can tell you about them, and you can buy them in any shop. A string of beads—thirty-three of them—stands for the thirty-three years of our Lord's life. If you're worried, the idea is to finger them; they're supposed to calm you down. The cab drivers have them hanging up in the windshields of their cars. Worry beads. What a comfort.

"Grudge beads" are just as effective. We can collect hurt feelings, like beads, and put them on a string. And we go over each bead, remembering this insult, that betrayal, this slight. What pleasure. We were put down by the unworthy and unwashed. Or better still, we were put down by our own brother. How virtuous it makes us feel.

Now grudges must be nourished if they are to stay alive. We must water them with our tears or they will shrivel and die. If we are practiced grudge collectors, we are hardly out of bed in the morning before we start fingering our grudge beads and begin our endless rounds. The idea is to never skip a bead, never to part with a single grudge. For every grudge kept nourished and alive and healthy helps to keep our image of ourselves intact.

And implicit in this little ritual is retaliation. One way or another, we'd love to "get even." It can range from out and out malice to just wanting to "get this thing resolved" (in some way so we'll come out smelling like a rose).

Grudge-holding can be a life-ruining habit. King David's son Absalom had a run-in with his father once and had to flee from home. But though his father David could forgive and forget, Absalom could not. His one goal in life was to get even with his father. And years later, when he finally did march against his father, David's orders to his soldiers were "deal gently with Absalom"—but Absalom's only thought was to "get my father."

And so Absalom's life was a total loss; he could not let go of his grudge.

Leo Tolstoy's marriage was a saga of bitterness. His wife carped and complained and clung to her grudges until he could not bear the sight of her. When they were married almost half a century, sometimes she would implore him to read to her the exquisite, poignant love passages that he had written about her in his diary forty-eight years previously, when they were both madly in love with each other. And as he read of the happy days that were now gone forever, they both wept bitterly.

Or you can put it in its place. If you give your hurts and injustices to God, they'll diminish in size; He'll give you the proper perspective. If you keep them, they'll stay big and ominous and ugly, or even grow more formidable with age.

Some psychiatric patients were allowed to go for holidays once, and each of them returned with practically the same story. Each had gone back for the first time to visit the place where he'd spent the first years of his life. Each of them strolled around the neighborhood and through his old home and re-visited the things that had terrorized and frustrated him. One had always thought his living room was the biggest room in the world, overpowering and frightening. But when he stepped into it again he found it was a room so small you could hardly turn around in it. The other remembered a deep and treacherous cliff near his house—he had always been terrified of it. But when he walked up to it again he found it was but a small ravine with a pitiful trickle of water at its base. Another remembered teachers in grades one to three who had awed her out of her wits. But when she talked to neighbors who had known them, she found they'd been mild-mannered and kind.*

Do you have any old grudges lying around? Then think on these verses:

Leviticus 19:18 "Thou shalt not avenge, nor bear any grudge against the children of thy people, but thou shalt love thy neighbor as thyself: I am the LORD."

Proverbs 20:22 "Say not thou, I will recompense evil; but wait on the LORD, and he shall save thee."

Proverbs 24:29 "Say not, I will do so to him as he hath done to me: I will render to the man according to his work."

Romans 12:17 "Recompense to no man evil for evil. Provide things honest in the sight of all men." (KJV)

Whether you are working on overt revenge or just fondling your grudge beads, you are wasting a lot of steam that could be put to better use.

"I've had it; I can't go another step!"

Now James is saying, "Be patient when things get rough."

*Distributed 1968 by Publishers-Hall Syndicate, L. A. Times.

The kind of patience he is writing about in verses 10 and 11 is the old "staying power" he mentioned in the first chapter.

Any athlete knows that all his natural gifts and know-how will do him no good if he does not develop stamina. Even our astronauts, with brains like computers and nerves of steel, need that magic ingredient.

Air Force Sergeant Joe Garnio has been with our astronauts since the first group was at Langley Air Force Base, Va., in 1960. He was a technical man assigned to care for their flight suits, oxygen equipment and other necessary gear. But Joe also had a background of knowledge about the human body under all kinds of stress. He knew from experience the benefits of rigorous physical training. And he knew that the deepest need of any person embarking on a difficult task was *stamina*. So he fixed up a one-room makeshift exercise center and they went to work. There was no rest for them, even in space. They exercised with a "bungee cord," hooking it around their feet, pulling against it, and giving their large leg and back muscles a workout. Even after fourteen days of immobility, except for the bungee cord—they returned to earth in splendid condition.

Stamina, staying power, endurance—call it what you will. It is as necessary in the spiritual realm as it is in the physical.

James gives us Job for an example. Now we cannot think of Job without thinking of patience, and it conjures up a picture of Job groveling, cringing, contemplating his loss of wealth, the death of his children, to say nothing of his boils—without so much as a sigh. Nothing could be farther from the truth. He cried out against his fate with passionate resentment, with questioning, and even with defiance. In Chapter 23 he cried "Oh that I knew where I might find him [God] . . . I would order my cause before him, and fill my mouth with arguments." Job exploded with arguments, but *he never lost his faith!* From his first self-assertiveness "My righteousness I hold fast, and will not let it go" (Job 27:6), to the moment of truth "I abhor myself, and repent in dust and ashes" (Job 42:6) he was a bundle of questions. But the big thing to remember about Job is that through it all he never lost his grip on God. Just as strong as the questions, was the cry "I know that my redeemer liveth" (19:25)! and "Though he slay me, yet will I trust in him" (13:15). Job did not have a groveling, passive patience. He had a gallant vibrant dynamic spirit.

Cut out the double talk

[12]"It is of the highest importance, my brothers, that your speech should be free from oaths (whether they are 'by' Heaven or earth or anything else). Your yes should be a plain yes, and your no a plain no, and then you cannot go wrong in the matter."

Oath taking was a common practice in those days. Men swore oaths for every transaction from the most important to the most trivial; it was the thing to do. And among the Jews, if God's name was used, the oath was binding; if God's name was not used the oath was worthless.

Now you can see the possibilities here at once. The idea was to be clever enough to imply that God was in it without actually using His name. Men became experts on circumlocution when it came to swearing oaths. Of course it got to the point of the ridiculous in time; and an oath did not mean a thing. It was like saying "I cross my heart and hope to die" when you were a kid—with your fingers crossed behind your back.

Jesus went into the matter in greater detail: "Don't use an oath at all. Don't swear by Heaven for it is God's throne; nor by the earth for it is his footstool; nor by Jerusalem for it is the city of the great king. No, and don't swear by your own head, for you cannot make a single hair—white or black! Whatever you have to say let your 'yes' be a plain 'yes' and your 'no' be a plain 'no'—anything more than this has a taint of evil" (Matthew 5:34-37). Which took care of every possibility the oath-swearers could conceivably think up to skirt the issue!

It's not the oath—it's the chap behind it

Yes. It was not the oath that counted back in those days—it was the *character of the person who made it*. And it still holds true today.

And what does all this boil down to? Exactly what James has been writing about practically since he started the letter! *Say what you mean and mean what you say!* This one great concept has threaded its way through every page. It has been implied in almost every issue James has brought up. Don't just "go through motions." Don't be a phony. Remember the Zenith slogan: "The quality goes in before the label goes on."

183

Your Christianity stands or falls on this question:
IS YOUR FAITH A HUMBUG OF
RELIGIOUS JARGON?
OR IS IT CHRIST IN YOU, *LIVING* IN YOU
BY THE POWER OF THE HOLY SPIRIT?

Think

1. Is there any such thing as a harmless grudge? Isn't it harmless as long as you keep it to yourself?

2. Memorize one of the verses under the heading: "Do you have any old grudges hanging around?"

3. How is your staying power? Remember Galatians 6:9. *"Let us not grow tired of doing good, for, unless we throw in our hand, the ultimate harvest is assured."* In this connection, read Hebrews 12:1.

4. Look up "humbug" in the dictionary and examine yourself in the light of the definition.

12

Why pray
when you can bungle?

Some wag said this. And as Christians, we can chuckle at it for we know it is ridiculous and we get the point at once. But the tragedy is, we go on living our lives as if we believed it. There isn't anything in James' letter that we could not somehow bungle our own way through and "get by," sometimes even seeming to come out on top of it all. We seem to have a built-in "I'd rather do it myself!" complex. So why pray?

James has some very definite things to say about prayer, and they cover just about everything we are apt to try to bungle through.

James 5:13-18

[13]"If any of you is in trouble let him pray. If anyone is flourishing let him sing praises to God. [14]If anyone is ill he should send for the church elders. They should pray over him, anointing him with oil

in the Lord's name. ¹⁵Believing prayer will save the sick man; the Lord will restore him and any sins that he has committed will be forgiven. ¹⁶You should get into the habit of admitting your sins to one another, and praying for one another, so that if sickness comes to you you may be healed.

¹⁶"Tremendous power is made available through a good man's earnest prayer. ¹⁷Do you remember Elijah? He was a man like us but he prayed earnestly that it should not rain. In fact, not a drop fell on the land for three and a half years. ¹⁸Then he prayed again; the heavens gave the rain and the earth sprouted with vegetation as usual."

Exactly what is prayer?

The great overall (and overwhelming!) concept of prayer is that Almighty God, who holds the universe in His hand, wants fellowship with *you*. Combine all the characteristics and all the particulars of prayer and they boil down to this one stunning fact. God wants to talk to *you*, listen to *you*, *be with you!* Under what circumstances? Under *all* circumstances. In trouble, in happy times, when you're ill, when you're well, when you're grateful and when you're not, and indeed, when there seems to be nothing to pray about at all. You have access to Him at all times. He wants to have access to you at all times. Does this seem unreasonable?

Think of your human relationships. When you love someone, you don't say "I love you. We'll keep in touch occasionally. I'll call you from time to time when I'm in trouble." Or, "I love you. Now don't bother me for awhile until I feel like contacting you

188

again; I'm so terribly busy." Or, "I love you. But I don't want to hear much about what you've done or what you're thinking." Or, "Don't call me, I'll call you."

Yet we do this very thing with God. We run to Him when we feel like it or when we're in trouble. Or we make out our prayer requests and problems like a shopping list and leave them hastily at His door—then pick them up again and run on our busy ways. For at certain stages of our Christian life we are apt to be a bit nervous about God and afraid He might not be quite up to it.

WE LEAVE OUR PRAYER REQUESTS AND PROBLEMS AT HIS DOOR...

THEN... PICK THEM UP AGAIN...

...AND RUN ON OUR BUSY WAYS

In verse 13, James says: "If any of you is in trouble let him pray." In the word "trouble" James is thinking of the things he has already written about: persecution, injustices, old fears, problems and all the gnats that plague us. These are the things you pray about during your quiet time, at odd moments during the day, when you have to cope with your tormentors (and when you don't)— And in the second part of the verse: "If anyone is flourishing let him sing praises to God"—he does not mean singing only, although this is certainly a part of it. He is speaking of an *attitude*, and this should certainly be constant. The idea is, you don't leave this attitude back there with your Bible; it goes with you, out of your prayer closet and into your very life.

But I can't spend my life on my knees!

No, but you can spend a part of it on your knees —not once a week or every time the mood seizes you, but some part of each day. Your spiritual vitality and spiritual health depend upon prayer and meditation on God's Word. It is your spiritual *food*. If we all made a pact with ourselves that we would go without eating every day we went without our quiet time, the whole problem would be ironed out in no time at all and there would be nothing more to say about it.

"But what is 'quiet time'? And how much is required? And how should I go about it?" Quiet time is just time spent alone with God. How it got the name of "quiet time" is a mystery for it need not be quiet at all. Some of it should be. ("Be still and know that I am God.") It's a good idea to lay aside

the "shopping list" and just kneel quietly before
God in an attitude of worship and thanksgiving.
But John Welch, one of the giants of the reforma-
tion, spent some of his quiet time pacing the floor,
talking aloud to God. A guest in his house once
woke in the night and heard talking in Welch's
room, and thought it so spooky, he tiptoed to
Welch's door and listened. He heard "conversation
between man and God such as he'd never dreamed
possible." And he stumbled into Welch's room and
begged to know the secret. How could anyone
know God as intimately as Welch seemed to?

How should I go about it? Your quiet time will
develop according to your own personality and
your own needs. To force yourself to read a given
amount of verses and then just kneel there, determined to stay a given length of time is doing it the
hard way. Go to God knowing that "the eyes of the
Lord are over the righteous, and his ears are open
unto their prayers" (I Peter 3:12, KJV). Go to your
quiet time expecting to meet your Lord. Remember
the hymn—"Beyond the sacred page I seek *Thee*,
Lord," and you'll go with a purpose, not just a
vague and sterile idea of "now it's time for devo-
tions." Go with your Bible and a planned reading
schedule and yes, a notebook. (All right, you may
never use it; but on the other hand you may find it
indispensable to jog your memory, to jell things—
just try it and see!)

You have a problem? Perhaps it would help you
to write it down. Make two columns, a pro and a
con, and lay the thing out before your Lord. Show
Him your pros and cons and tell Him you want to

191

know His will in the matter. As you read your Bible and as you pray, you'll find yourself scratching out pros or cons, until one or the other is scratched out completely. Dr. Alan Redpath did this when he felt God calling him into the ministry. It took a year before the cons were all gone and he was absolutely sure. A *year*? Yes. It was a monumental decision and he did not want to make a mistake.*

There's a crisis? In the Chinese language, the word "crisis" is made up of two other words, one of which means "problem" and the other "opportunity." Go to your Lord with your crisis. Ask Him to show you the opportunity. The crisis may uncover a life-changing opportunity for you to act upon. Or it may afford an opportunity to be patient and exercise your faith for the moment, until He shows you how he is going to work it out.

There's no big problem, no big crisis—just a lot of messy little issues all fogged up and not worth bothering Him with? Go to Him with just that— *telling* Him your life is cluttered up with just a lot of messy little issues all fogged up and not worth bothering Him with. If you mean business, you'll feel a sense of His love, His caring, and no issue will be too trivial to take to Him.

There never seems to be an answer, a sense of His presence? Perhaps you've got the order wrong. First, worship. Worship is "reverent honor and homage paid to God." Then thanksgiving. This means when you don't feel like it, and when there

---

Getting to Know the Will of God, Alan Redpath, Inter-Varsity Press, Chicago.

doesn't seem to be anything in your circumstances to be thankful for. Thank Him for *Himself*. Then confession. And implicit in confessing is the idea that you are going to *do* something about it.

(And when you have done something about it and the sin is forgiven and forsaken, forget it. Don't keep digging it up. The tendency to think that "God has forgiven me but I can't shake the idea that He's still a little mad at me" is verboten.)

Then intercession for others. And this does not mean just to tell Him to "straighten the other fellow out." It means to ask for others with the same love and concern that you feel when you ask for yourself. *Then,* your own petitions for yourself.

How much time is required? The closer you are to God, the less inclined you will be to ask this question. Start out with the idea that you are just going to meet with God each day—with your Bible and your notebook. Just that, no more. (If the notebook remains empty, don't worry about it; it isn't important.) And that's absolutely the only rule you need to start with. If you really mean business, and you discipline yourself to do just this much, you'll find your time with God getting longer without your knowing. The better you know your Lord, the more things there are to talk about! You'll find yourself putting more and more details of your life into His hands. And you'll find yourself using that notebook. And the jottings in your Bible margins will increase. And then you'll find yourself talking to Him at odd moments throughout your day, almost without thinking—it will be as natural as breathing.

And there will be times when your Lord is more real to you than any person. *Any* person. How much time is *required?* The word "require" will drop right out of your thinking. You'll be doing it because you want to. You will "pray without ceasing" (I Thessalonians 5:17). Your life will be an *attitude* of prayer.

Praying in public. Sometimes it seems that this is the easiest thing to do. We do it glibly in meetings, using fine phrases and spiritual cliches, sometimes running our words in together without thought or meaning — "DearHeavenlyFatherwetrulythankThee for—" and when we finish we don't know what we've said and neither does anybody else. There isn't any one of us who hasn't been guilty of this at one time or another. The tragedy is when we allow it to become a habit.

Or we keep quiet, not daring to open our mouths because others seem to be so good at it we're afraid of making ourselves look ridiculous. And sometimes those of us who keep quiet are at least as sincere as those who are praying. There was a boy once, who could never pray when his high school group did. But one night they "prayed around the circle" and he realized he was not about to get out of it. The time came, inexorably, closer and closer to him and he absolutely panicked. And then he did something that shocked the group right out of its complacency. He blurted out, "O God—I just don't know how to pray aloud. I've never been able to get the hang of it. I love You, Lord, and I really want to be able to pray like the others do. But You'll just have to help me." And he proceeded to pour out a prayer in his own words, and it was so stumbling, so sincere, so honest and so completely *refreshing* that he stopped the little prayer meeting in its tracks. There was a long pause when he finished. And then those who prayed after him completely forgot all the neat little stereotyped prayers they'd made up to say and *they* began to just pour out their hearts to God in the same simple way he had done. Pat prayers went down the drain. And the amazing part of the story is that it didn't stop there. Something had happened! The whole evening went better. They all went home feeling that in some inexplicable way they'd really met God head-on, they'd come to grips with the elusive thing they'd always in the past somehow missed. But it didn't stop *there*. The next Sunday night, they asked this boy to *start* the prayer time, in a sense, to teach *them* how to pray. He did, and again the effect was electric. The upshot of a long story was that they began to have Saturday morning prayer meetings. Then they put legs on their prayers and began to act, to produce, to bear fruit, to obey—and to set that church afire! Things were never the same with that group of high schoolers from the moment one scared guy admitted that he did not know how to pray, and asked God to teach him.

Let's get down to specifics: what about my life?

The most precious gift God has given you is your life. And now, as a Christian, your new life in Christ. As James said in Chapter 4, you have no promise of how long it is going to be. But you do have the prerogative to choose what you are going to do with it. It is unthinkable that you would make this all-important choice without God.

All things being equal, the two most important decisions you are going to make in your life are (1) what you are going to choose for your career and (2) who you are going to choose to marry. If you leave God out of either of these decisions, you will bungle through a second-rate course that will be like an obstacle race, and you will wind up like a white mouse in a laboratory cage, in a maze of corridors and blind alleys that lead nowhere. What a gross injustice to do yourself! It's like starting out on the track with your legs bundled in a potato sack. Because He has given you this awesome power of free will, you can literally deprive Him of the power to carry out His best plan for your life!

Bill Glass,* All-American pro football player, prayed definitely about his life, in college. But he'd been thinking about God, and God's will for his life, ever since high school.

In college, a friend came to him and said, "Bill, you're an average football player, but you could be worlds better. You have the physical equipment to be a great football player. God could widen your Christian testimony as a result of it. You've been playing fairly good football. But honestly, Bill, you've just been mediocre. So, if you can play inspired football amazing things can happen."

They began to pray.

Three days before they were to go to the West Coast to play the University of California, they

*Get in the Game by Bill Glass, Word Publishers.

were in prayer. And Bill's friend became so bold as to say, "Let's pray *specifically* that you may become an All-American and that as an All-American, you may use whatever glory this honor brings you to the glory of God."

Bill Glass says, "During this prayer meeting we had a peculiar awareness of God's presence. With these challenging thoughts and convictions before us, we rose to our feet with the realization that something big might happen."

Something big *did* happen, and "big" things have been happening to Bill Glass ever since. But the important thing is this. Bill tells it: "My zeal for Christ was restored through the constant remembrance of the very real and vivid conversion I had experienced *in high school,* the realization of God's presence in my life, and the answers to prayer that I continued to have."

Bill was serious about choosing a mate too. And it wasn't one of those nebulous "I'll fool around for awhile and then, when I get around to it, I'll ask God about who to marry" sort of things. Let's see what he has to say about it:

"During my high school years I dated some, but football kept me so busy I just didn't have time to 'go out' a lot. It was different when I got to college. My interest in girls accelerated. I dated lots of girls, but I never seriously contemplated marrying any of them. The first time, I guess, that I really thought seriously about marriage was during my senior year. I had a very idealistic view of marriage. I felt that my future wife would be a Christian, that we would have a great deal in common, and that she would be a wonderful person. I don't know why, but I thought she'd be a freshman. I knew that marriage would be a serious step and I made it a matter of prayer . . . not constantly, of course, for I didn't think I was that close to it, but there were many times when I did ask God to have His will about *who I dated and ultimately married.*"

Then he goes on to say—"I heard by the campus grapevine that Mavis Knapp, a cute little brunette (a freshman, by the way) wanted to meet me. I thought that she must be out of her head and I really didn't feel that anything would come of it. But if she really wanted to date me, and if she were as cute as they said, I couldn't see any reason why I shouldn't accommodate her."

On their first date, he was going out to speak at a church, and he asked her if she could sing or play the piano. He figured if she were going along she might as well be of some use. She could do neither.

"I thought she was hilarious," he says. "Right off, on our second date, she told me she felt she wanted to marry a person like me. I was amazed and thought, I really picked a dumb freshman this time."

But it turned out that she was utterly sincere in what she felt to be God's will for her. He says, "If God had inititated her interest in someone like me, who was I to argue?"

But the important thing about this little tale is that *he continued to seek God's will for their friendship.* "I began to feel," he says, "that God had destined us for each other, but I didn't know why. How was I to know that she was to be the greatest thing that ever happened to me? I have often looked back in wonder at why I had the growing certainty that the relationship between Mavis and me was a part of God's plan for our lives. Her background was the same as mine."

Well it turned out that she *was* the "greatest thing that had ever happened to him."

The crux of the matter is that he did not choose to "fool around for awhile" and get around to God's will for his life when he felt like it. He was tremendously *interested* in God's will for his life from the beginning. And he did not wind up in a trap with every road leading to a blind alley. God is able to do His best for Bill, because Bill *chose* God's best.

Is healing for real?

Among Christians, there is as much confusion about health and sickness as there is about wealth or poverty. If you're always well and healthy you "must have done something good." And if you're stricken with any serious illness, God is furious with you and you are being punished.

This confusion is topped only by the mixed feelings about God's healing. If you pray and do get healed, you must be very spiritual (or somebody is sure to tell you it would have happened anyway whether you prayed or not). And if you don't get healed, you either didn't have enough faith or you still have secret sins in your life. In all this theorizing, we leave out one great overwhelming fact—the *sovereignty of God.*

Jesus went about healing indiscriminately, or so it seems, both the worthy and the unworthy: those with boundless faith and those with very little or none at all.

Paul, one of the greatest giants in faith who ever lived, beseeeched God to heal him of his "thorn in the flesh" and God did not. On the other hand, there was probably no man on earth who went for healing with as wrong an attitude as Naaman (II Kings 5:1-19) the leper. When Elijah told him to go bathe in the Jordan, he was scandalized. What? In the muddy old Jordan? He had nicer rivers in his own country! He was about to drive off in a snit, and his servants had to beg him to at least give God a try. When he did, and he was healed of his leprosy, he was absolutely speechless. He'd had no faith at all; he'd approached God like a pompous ass. And God (through Peter) healed a lame man at the door of the Temple, who had not even *asked* to be healed; he'd been asking for money.

"But those were in Bible times. What about now? Does God still heal?" Of course He does! The cases of miraculous healing that are on record are plentiful, authenticated, documented. And where does this leave us? Right back with the sovereignty of God.

Are you concerned for yourself? Your friend? (Remember the four men who took their friend to Jesus, could not get near Him because of the crowds, cut a hole in the roof, and lowered him down to Jesus' very feet?) You have every right to ask for your own healing or the healing of your friend. And of course sin should be confessed and made right, but you just don't bargain with God. ("I've made everything all right, confessed my sins, and I have enough faith—so now heal me.") Your first concern is *the will of God for your life.*

Dr. S. I. McMillen says, "Peace does not come in capsules! This is regrettable because medical science recognizes that emotions such as fear, sorrow, envy, resentment and hatred are responsible for the majority of our sicknesses."*

Ask God to heal you of your critical spirit, your slippery tongue, your capacity for holding a grudge, your dishonesty both with yourself and with Him. And if any of these faults are hurting another, admit it and make it right (verse 16). Admitting faults to one another does not mean unbridled and hurtful dredging up of sins that are between you and God.

And your physical malady? Ask Him, of course. But remember Chapter 4. "If God *wants* me to, I shall do such and such." If you make your everyday plans according to His will, then surely you must leave your healing with Him. It all goes together or it all falls apart. If you have asked healing for yourself or your friend and it does not come about, don't punish yourself and don't let others punish you. Your life is in God's hands. If you are all right with Him, pick yourself up and go on rejoicing. Your life with God is a great adventure, whether or not you are healed!

Satan would have a word with thee

Satan has a word to say to you concerning prayer. *Don't.* He will allow you all sorts of other spiritual indulgences—going to meetings, reading Christian

---

*None of These Diseases, S. I. McMillen. Fleming H. Revell Co., New Jersey.

literature, giving your testimony—but prayer? Out, out, out! Of course, pat little prayers are all right. The prayers rattled off in monotonous rote, or intoned in acceptable sing-song rhythm, very pretty and signifying nothing, do not bother him a bit. He would just as soon you *did* indulge in that kind of praying; it's a sop to your conscience and could conceivably keep you in a spiritual stupor for the rest of your life. It does him no harm and does you no good. But he will do anything to keep you from fervent earnest prayer, inspired and empowered by the Holy Spirit, honest and gut-level. This sort of praying terrifies him. "Satan trembles when he sees the weakest Christian on his knees" has been said so much it's threadbare but it is still true.

In Bunyan's *Holy War*, Satan admonishes his demons: "Mind you, don't get careless. Watch what these Christians do to relieve their misery. Drive them to complaining, drive them to quarreling, drive them to anything but petitions! And if I so much as catch one of them—just *one* of them on his knees—" The demons would tremble at the very thought. "Back down in the bottomless pit you go!" he would shriek. "By my own hand. I'll toss you there myself!"

It was not the thought of petitions that worried him; as long as they were spurious or purely emotional or halfhearted or sporadic he had nothing to fear. It was the thought of petitions sent through the Holy Spirit of God that made him tremble.

If you've gotten the victory in this business of praying regularly and in earnest, you are off to a good start, but Satan is not through with you; you have just won the first skirmish. He can still make mischief, even while you are on your knees. His taunts are unlimited, but here are a few:

"You've already asked Him about this matter; it's obvious He does not intend to do a thing. Why don't you give up?" This is a standard taunt, Satan's answer to importunity.

"There's still some secret sin in your life He hasn't revealed to you yet." This is more subtle and a great one to send you off in a tizzy of morbid introspection, taking your spiritual temperature every few hours, and getting so absorbed in yourself that you are rendered quite ineffective.

"Oh, come *on* now, you aren't going to have the unmitigated gall to ask Him to forgive you for that one *again*. You've fallen down on that one so many times it has become ridiculous. Don't you feel a bit foolish?" This is bound to make you feel like a real clod if you don't remember that you are depending on His absolute faithfulness; nobody ever said *you* were any great shakes in that department.

"You're getting to be quite spiritual, you know." This is calculated to throw you completely off your guard. If you're not very careful you'll be believing it in no time, and while you are outwardly forsaking all the more obvious sins, you will be inwardly fondly coddling a sin of your own—the sin of spiritual pride.

Then there are the more obvious taunts, not the least of which is "And do you really think God is interested in such trifles?" This one and its ilk should be ignored and considered beneath your contempt: There are enough real problems in prayer without your giving taunts like this the time of day.

Robert Murray McCheyne wrote: "For every look you take at yourself, take ten at Jesus Christ." Look at your Lord. Listen to your Lord. And when Satan plants a doubt or a hindrance in your mind, turn it over to your Lord at once, refuse to put up with it, dismiss it—and then *forget it*.

But I'm only me

"Aren't all the really big accomplishments in prayer for the 'spiritual giants'?" All right, who are the "spiritual giants"? James mentions Elijah (verses 17,18). The Bible is full of them. But in every case, they come to us in a package deal—their human frailties are included. A spiritual giant is an ordinary human being like yourself who has just taken God at His word. You have access to the same boundless power of the Holy Spirit of God as they did. A spiritual giant is *anybody*—plus God!

And in conclusion

James ends his letter with touching tenderness. It is so simple. He does not scold and he does not explain. But the teachings of the entire letter seem to be summed up in the last two verses:

[19]"My brothers, if any of you should wander away from the truth and another should turn him back on to the right path, [20]then the latter may be sure that in turning a man back from his wandering course

he has rescued a soul from death, and his living action will 'cover a multitude of sins.'"

JAMES

If your Christian friend loses the first joy of his salvation, stumbles into unbelief, into despondency, into indifference, into sin—you will never bring him back by criticism, by jealousy, by an attitude of self-righteousness—in short, *by being a phony*. You will bring him back by prayer, by concern, by love, by personal effort—by honesty and sincerity, knowing that we are all bundles of weaknesses ("Let him who thinks he stands, beware, lest he fall"). You will bring him back by living out the great social and moral and spiritual truths in this letter.

Don't be a phony. And if you are sharp enough to discern phoniness in others be mature enough to forgive them.

Surely this is your utmost—for your Lord.

Dear James,

I got your letter okay and I read every word. Well no, that's not quite true. Actually I just sort of flipped through it at first, skipping over the parts that didn't seem to apply to me. It *did* seem a bit choppy in spots. And frankly there were times when you just didn't seem to be with it and the generation gap really showed.

And then I began to read it, you know, really read it. And you began to really come through. And I was surprised to find that you jumped right over the credibility cutoff to where we are. You feel the same way about this phony business as we do and you're saying the same things we've been trying to get across. You might not say it in tne same way but you mean the same things. When it hit me that your letter was for *today* I really began to dig in. And I got to thinking about the fact that, in my own way, I might be a bit phony in spots too. There are all sorts of ways to be phony—everybody has his own thing.

Anyhow I began to think about the things you said and even began to work on some of them. Of course you brought me up with such a jolt right at the beginning that you almost didn't get the rest of your letter read (by me, that is). I've got problems? And I'm supposed to count them all *joy*? I can't find a word for me, sputtering, but that's what I'm doing. I will admit that I learned something about my problems I never knew before—you know, that they were to test my endurance and make my faith grow. It helps to know this, and I get the point all right. But I'll be hanged if I can count it all joy and I don't think I ever will. All I can say is, Job, move over.

About this business of temptation, I really thought you were putting me on at first. But I began to check myself and I had to admit that most of my temptations *do* strike an answering chord in me. I mean sometimes I'm actually just itching to be tempted. It's everything from sex to wearing a chip on my shoulder and hoping somebody will come along and knock it off so I can explode. And some of the sneaky shortcuts I've taken to reach some of my goals, just came up and hit me when I began to think about them and recognize them. Honestly, it was almost funny. I found myself laughing at myself over some of them. But some of them were no laughing matter.

I guess the greatest thing I got out of your letter was the idea that I had the power of choice. I can choose God or I can choose my own way. You know the fact that He loves me that much is sort of overwhelming. I knew Jesus died for me, to make it so I could come to terms with God, but I didn't act as if I knew it. I'd made a sort of commitment, but now I've made a more personal one, one that involved me and sort of scared me too. I don't know if I'm going to be up to it. It struck me while I was reading about temptation, that all of my life is a bunch of choices, really. From the minute you choose Jesus, you begin making choices in everything you do. It's Jesus or *it*, or Jesus or *him*, or Jesus or *me*. Golly.* I'll bet you never thought of that; you didn't mention it.

Your concept of freedom is terrific. The idea that the only real freedom is in being a Christian and accepting the will of God and obeying the law of God. Then I'm free to be the person I want to be? That's so absolutely way out that my mind can't get hold of it, but I'm working on it too. Naturally I want to believe it because it sounds so great, but it's one of those deals that will take a bit of practice and I imagine it will be awhile before I live it out and see what you're getting at.

I dug what you said about snobs. I was with you all the way. Right up until the concept of being a snob *about* snobs hit me. That's what I am! I'll give it some thought.

You said my faith is empty without good works

*You also said not to use God's name in vain. Sorry about that. I'm working on it.

and that sort of stopped me cold. The idea that any "do-gooder" can come along and make hash out of my testimony if I'm not living up to it! Wow. I might as well tell you that I haven't been living up to it. I'm not going to promise too much but I've made a few starts in different areas of my life.

This business of the tongue is a subject I'd just as soon skip. My only comfort is that I have lots of company. I think I veer between being a "fact-skipper" and a "fact-adder", myself. And when I do shut up I give with some of those looks. I didn't realize I could "talk without opening my mouth!"

Oh, about this wisdom idea. I thought I knew all about it—you know, learning facts and having enough know-how to apply them to my life and all. But you took it one step further. The idea that I can be applying the knowledge I've collected to my life *in utter confusion* is a pretty thought-provoking concept. Well, I've got a lot of facts knocking around in my head and I've worked hard to get them, so I'm inclined to go along with the idea that the wisdom of God is the way to go. You won't get any argument from me. Except for some of the characteristics of that kind of wisdom. Pure— gentle— peace-loving— courteous— and a lot of other stuff. If I really get all that I'll be too good for earth.

I never had any list of "do's and don'ts"—at least I didn't think I did. Until I began to examine my thinking. My face came out sort of red. Do you know I have my own little list of "do's and don'ts" that doesn't match anybody else's—it's just custom-made for me. And in my own way I'm as much of a spiritual snob as some of the snobs I can't stand!

I'm glad the Bible is full of stuff about laughter. God says some pretty good things about the "merry heart" that I sure go along with. Tears for repentance, yes—but going along in a gloom like some Christians do is not for me.

There's something you said that I don't like. And I don't think I ever will. Something about not making friends with the pleasures of this evil world. Getting it straight in my mind as to what pleasures are legitimate and what pleasures aren't is no small job. Like I said, everybody has his own thing. Something that's okay for me might make you go up like a rocket. I'll keep working on it.

As for making plans like there was no God—that scared me. Well it sobered me. The idea that I might not have even my next breath sort of stopped me cold. You don't have to like the idea but you sure can't ignore it. I find myself—well, I'm not going to go around chanting "the Lord willing" like some kind of a nut, but I find myself *thinking* it—and not with sadness, really. Along with the scary idea that you might die any time is the idea that you are so much in *God's* hands. Brother, it's a big concept.

So you had some strong feelings about money too? That's interesting, you know, because we feel the same way. I realize now, though, that you can't do *away* with money; it *is* here to stay. I'm going to try for a middle-of-the-road feeling about it—you know, take it or leave it; I don't want to get hung up on it.

I've never been a grudge collector, so that part

didn't hit me. I think that's a fault that older saints are more apt to be addicted to.

Hey, I looked up "humbug" in the dictionary and it means the same thing as "phoniness"! Was I surprised to find that out! I thought humbug was reserved for old Scrooge and that it meant—well I never thought much about what it meant. Is my faith a humbug of religious jargon—or is it Christ in me, living in me by the power of the Holy Spirit? Brother that's one to make me stop and think. I'm trying to count on the Holy Spirit and the whole idea gets easier—I mean I get more familiar with the fact that He really *is* in me and I have access to His power—anyhow I find the going easier as I go along. All of this sure isn't going to happen overnight, though, so don't anybody hold his breath.

I've never been very strong on the prayer life—never had a quiet time, actually. But now I've been trying it, since reading your letter. I understand that you were known as the "man with the camel's knees" so I won't argue with you about prayer. You sure must know what you're talking about. But do you know, I find myself just sort of *talking* to God, you know, inside my head. At odd moments. Even when there isn't anything to ask for. I don't know whether I'm going nuts or what. All I know is, I'm happy. I ask Him things like—well personal things. If it sounds dopey I don't care. He's closer to me than a lot of my friends are.

This whole concept of phoniness has been eluding me but I think I've got it figured out. I was always confused about it. I was never the kind of a nut who just said all adults were phony and just wrote them all off, or anything like that. Because I knew too many adults who *weren't* phony. And a lot of kids in my group who *were*. I think now that phoniness cuts across all barriers including the credibility cutoff—I mean right down through *everybody*. We're all made of "ticky-tacky" and we're all just the same. There are some phonies in every church. And some phoniness in *some* areas of *every* person's life. I've been liking more adults lately, I mean even some of the ghouley ones, since I realized this. And I think *I'm* a little easier to get along with. I think young people are more honest and more willing to face up to themselves these days. I mean it isn't fair to say they're just picking on adults and cutting them all up, because they're willing to look at themselves too.

Some hotshot wrote about "the pathetic meagerness of our media-created inner lives." I don't want this to happen to me. I know that even though I have the Holy Spirit inside me, in my personality and my heart—I can dry Him up or grieve Him or whatever it is you do. I don't want that. I'm beginning, just *beginning* to feel this new freedom you talked about—you know, the law of liberty in Christ.

There are some things I'm not ready to part with yet and some of the good things of God I don't even want. I don't know what that makes me, but at least I'm not going to be phony about it.

The idea of your calling yourself "servant of God and of the Lord Jesus Christ" really stops me. When you stop to think that it all must have happened— this transformation I mean—when Jesus appeared to you after His resurrection. "He was seen of James." Boy. Phew! Would I ever like to have seen *that!*

Thank you for your "great roaring letter," James. I don't like the term "practical Christianity" but I guess that's what your letter is about. Anyhow it sure ought to be read by every Christian every six months as a sort of a routine checkup.

Sincerely,

*

P.S. I don't expect to get "squeaky clean" overnight, and perhaps not ever, but one thing I've resolved to do. *Be honest.* I think I'd rather be an honest stumbling Christian than a phony "super-spiritual" one.

*If you agree, why not sign your name?